HOW TO DRAW DINOSAURS

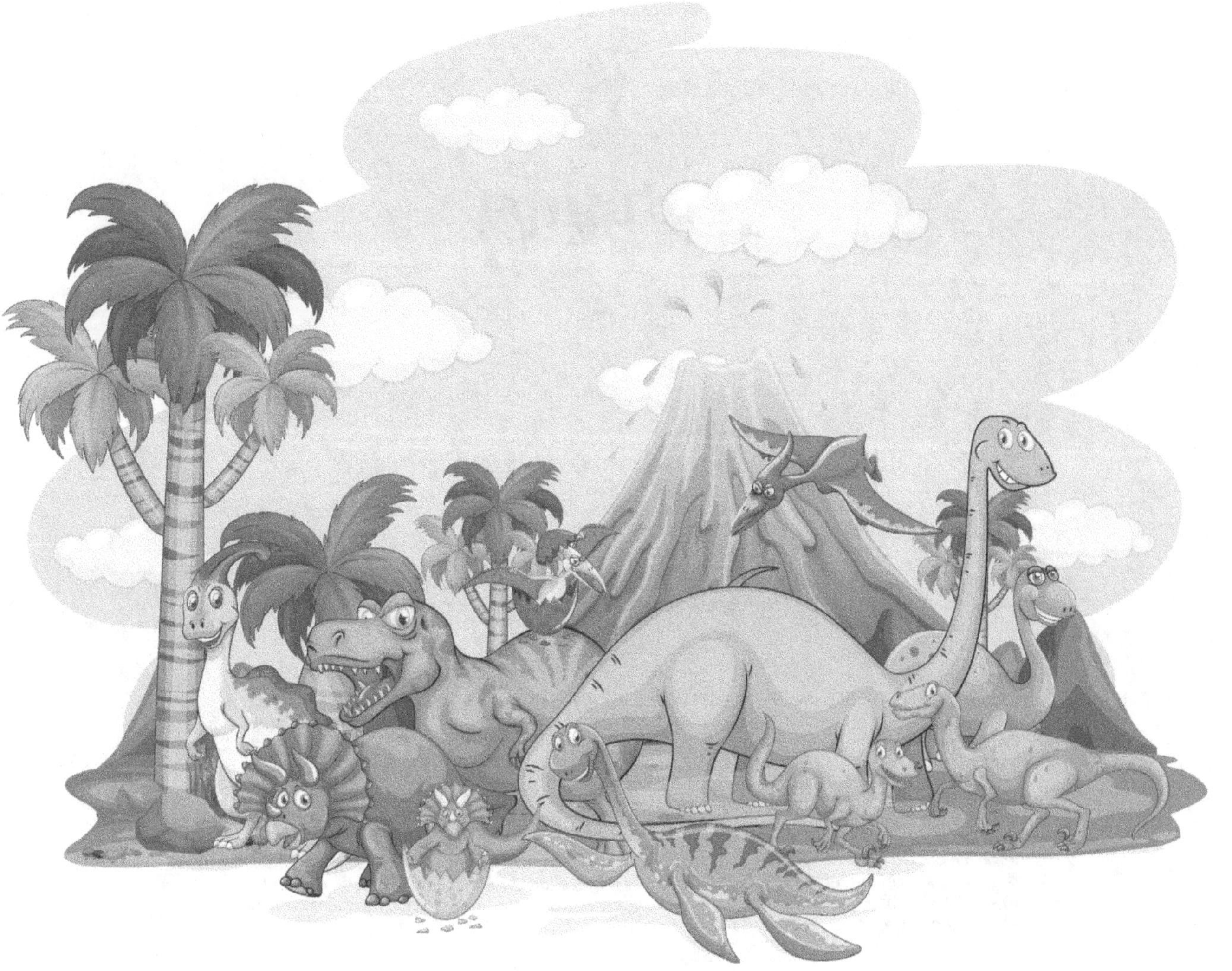

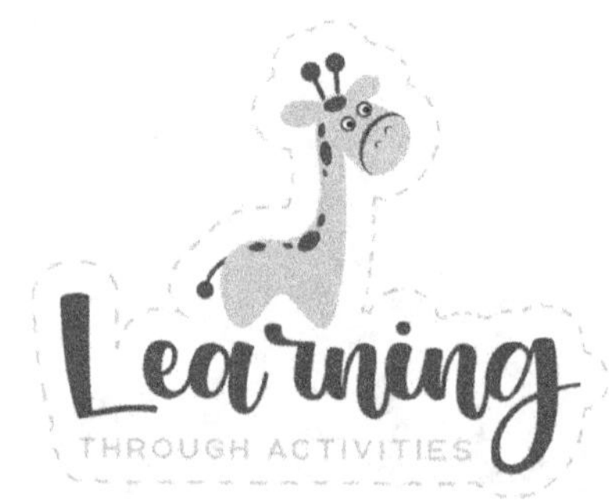

SPECIAL BONUS!

Want These 2 Books For FREE?

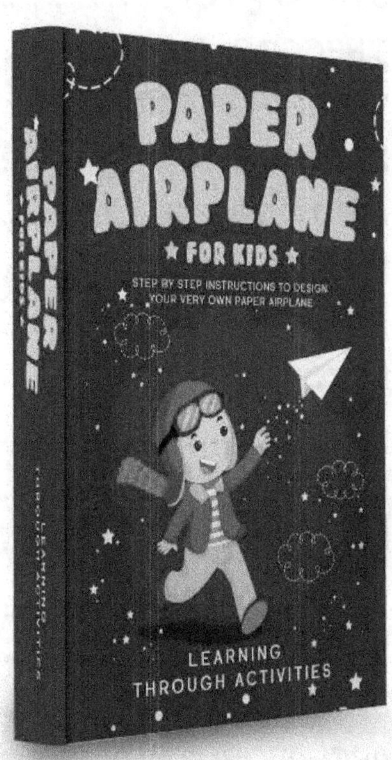

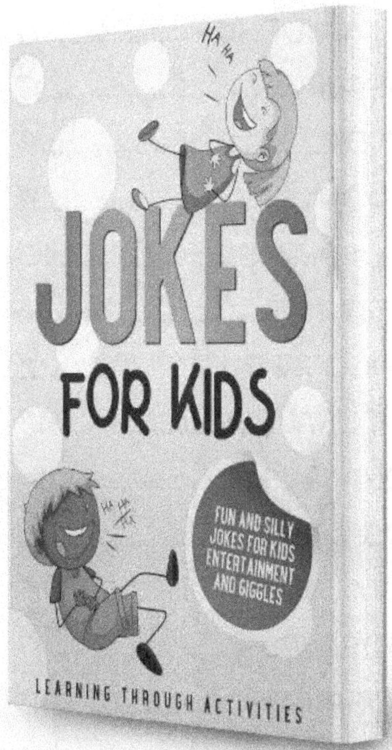

Get **FREE**, unlimited access to these and all of our new kids books by joining our community!

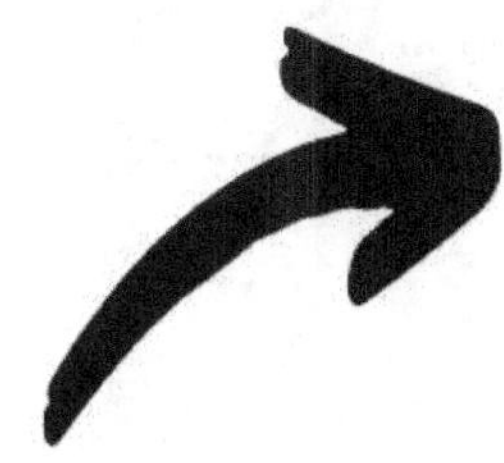

Scan W/ Your Camera To Join!

CONTENTS

INTRODUCTION

WELCOME TO 'HOW TO DRAW DINOSAURS.' THIS BOOK IS FULL OF ALL DIFFER-
ENT KINDS OF DINOSAURS THAT GO WAY, WAY BACK IN TIME!

EACH DINOSAUR HAS EASY TO FOLLOW INSTRUCTIONS THAT WILL STEP-BY-
STEP HAVE YOU DRAWING THEM LIKE A PRO! YOU'LL BE AN ARTIST BEFORE
YOU KNOW IT!

NOT ONLY WILL YOU LEARN HOW TO DRAW ALL OF THESE DINOSAURSS, YOU
WILL ALSO LEARN A FACT ABOUT EACH, WHERE IT WAS ORIGINATED AND THE
SPEED OR SIZE OF EACH DINOSAUR TOO!

PLEASE DON'T WORRY IF YOUR DINOSAURS TURN OUT A LITTLE DIFFERENT
FROM THE ONES IN THE PICTURES, WE ALL HAVE OUR UNIQUE STYLE, AND
ALSO, PRACTICE MAKES PERFECT!

GENERALLY, IT'S BEST TO START WITH A PENCIL WHILE YOU ARE GETTING THE
HANG OF IT, SO LITTLE MISTAKES CAN BE EASILY ERASED. THEN MOVE ONTO
PENS, COLORED, SPARKLY, WHATEVER YOU LIKE.
HAVE FUN!

STEGOSAURUS

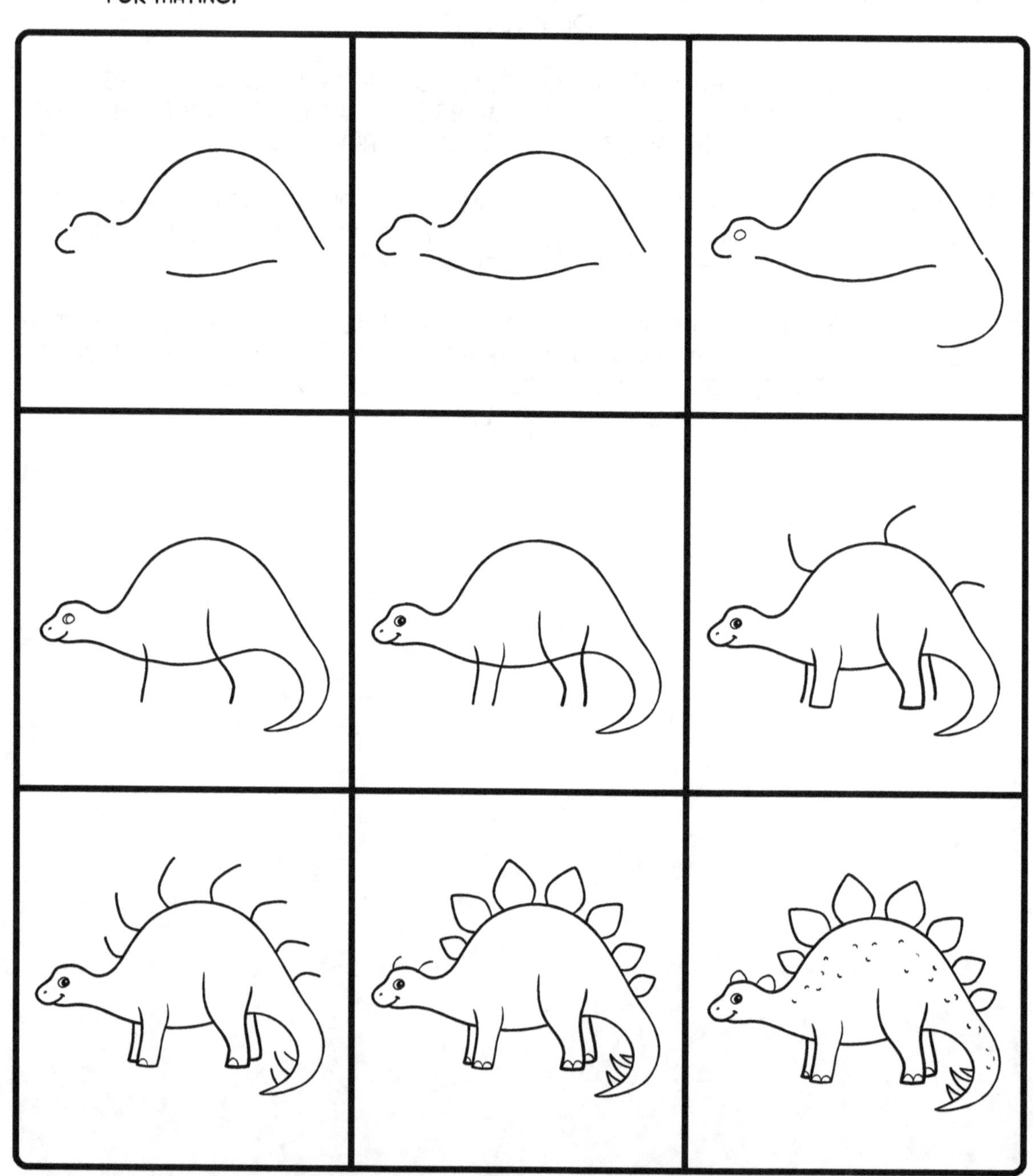

PARASAUROLOPHUS

FACT:

HAS A TUBE-LIKE CREST THAT IT USES TO MAKE ITS BEAUTIFUL HAUNTING CRIES.

SIZE:

16 FEET – ALMOST AS TALL AS A GIRAFFE.

ORIGIN:

UTAH/NEW MEXICO

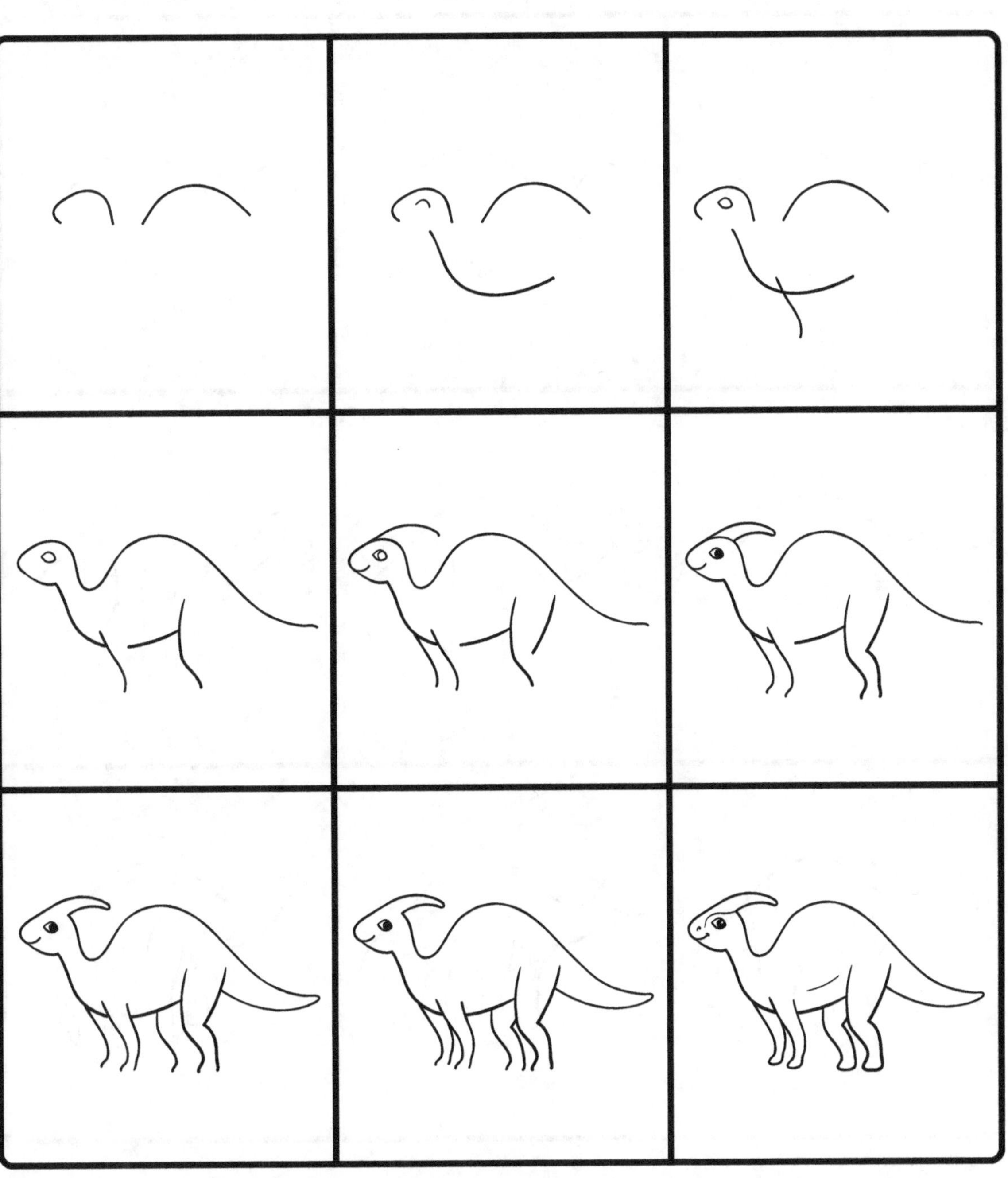

TITANOSAURUS

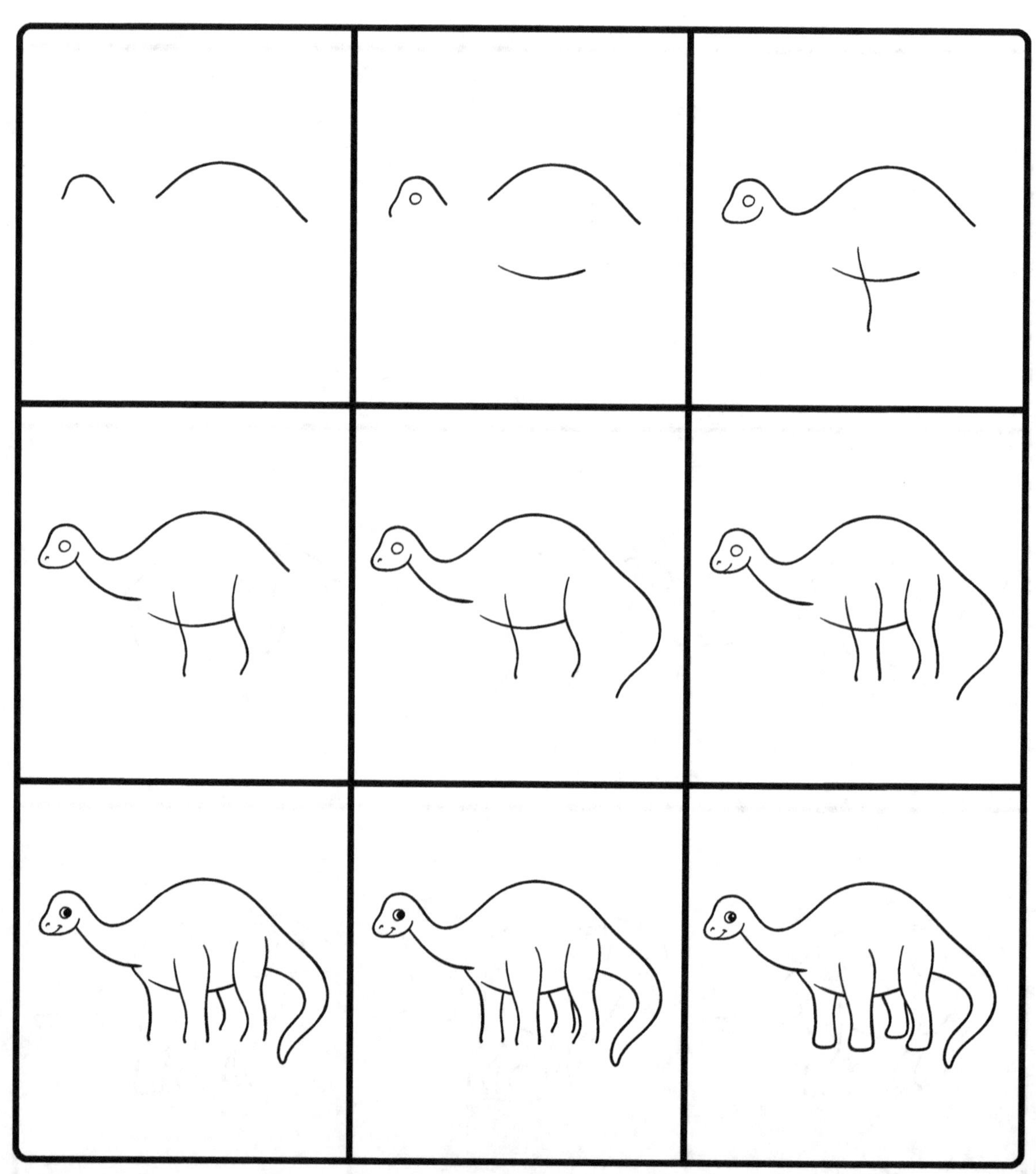

OUIRAPTOR

FACT:
THEIR NAME MEANS 'ROBBER OF EGGS,' BUT THEY DO NOT EVEN EAT EGGS!

SPEED:
42 MILES PER HOUR – AS FAST AS A CROW.

ORIGIN:
MONGOLIA

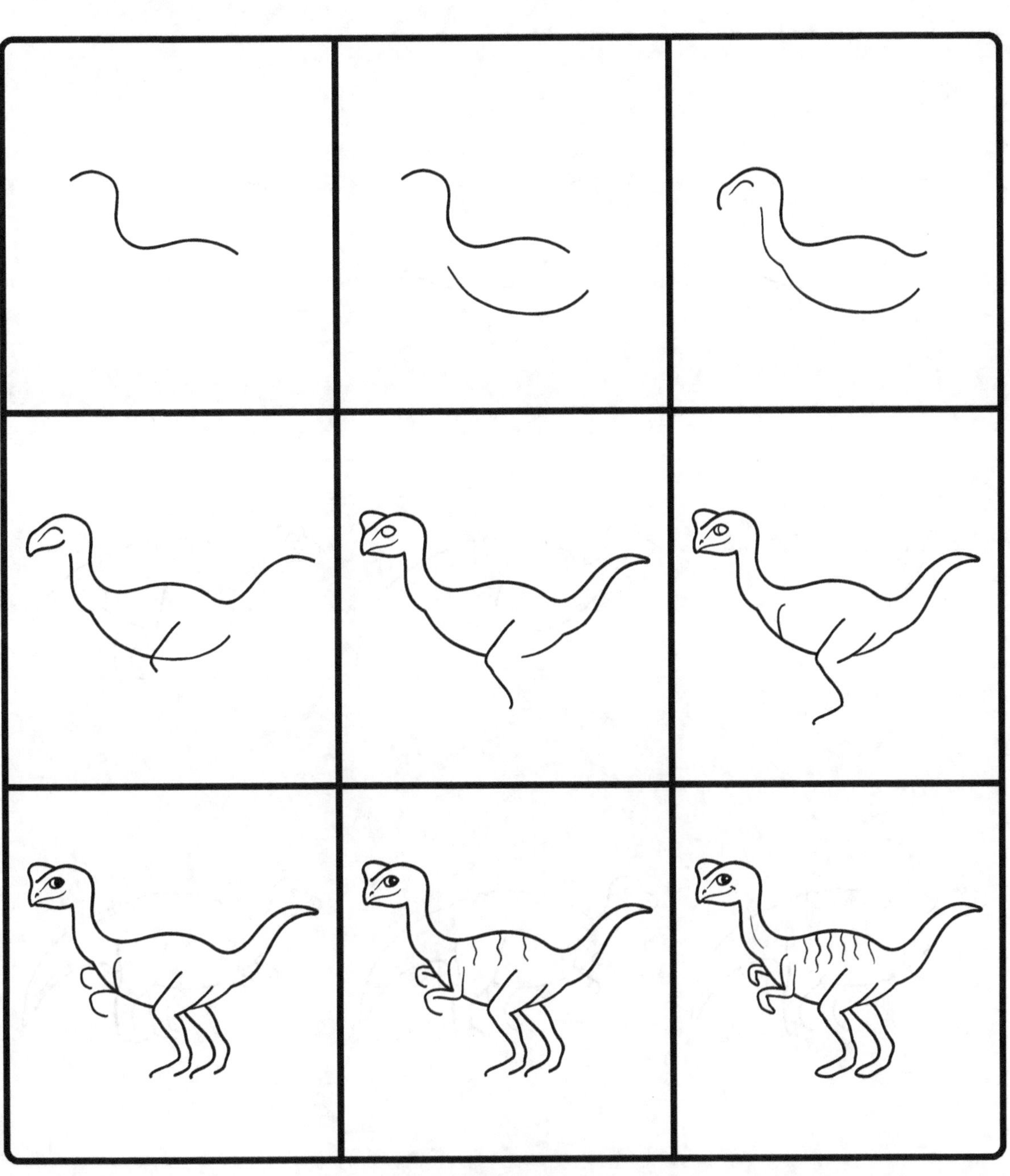

IGUANODON

FACT:
HAS AN INTERESTING THUMB SPIKE THAT IT USES FOR DEFENSE.

SPEED:
15 MILES PER HOUR - ALMOST AS FAST AS A POLAR BEAR.

ORIGIN:
BELGIUM

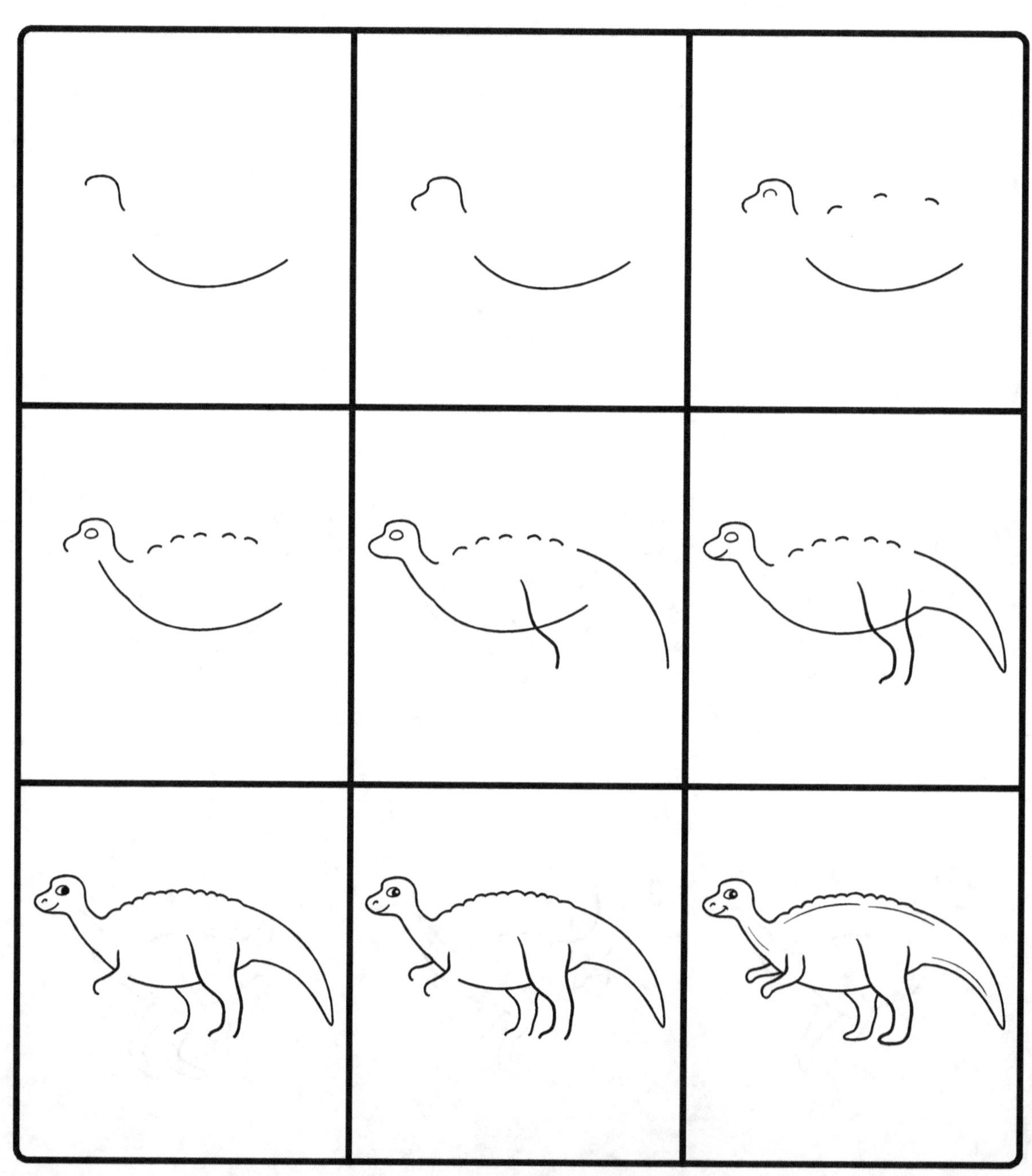

PANOPLOSAURUS

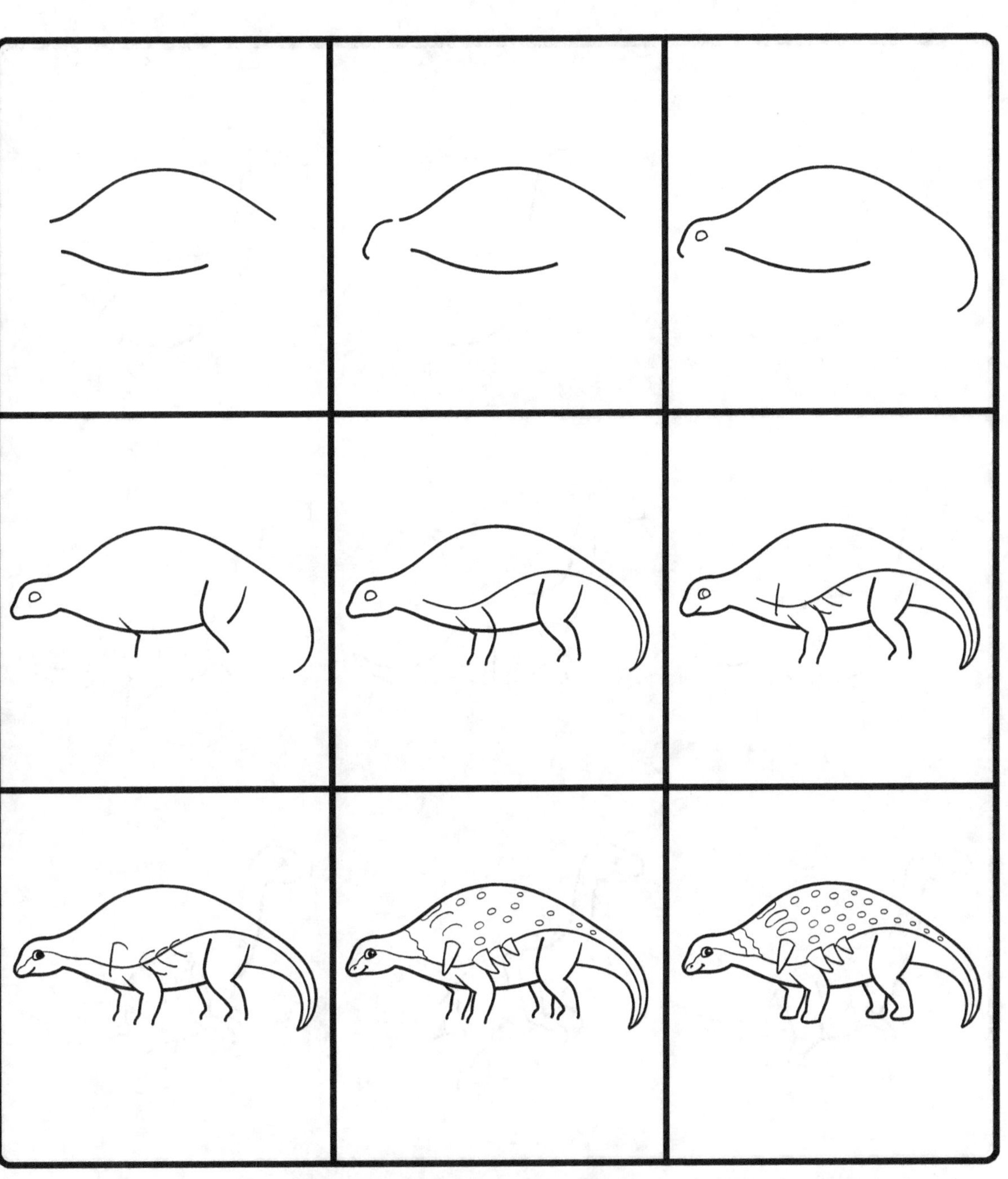

PLATEOSAURUS

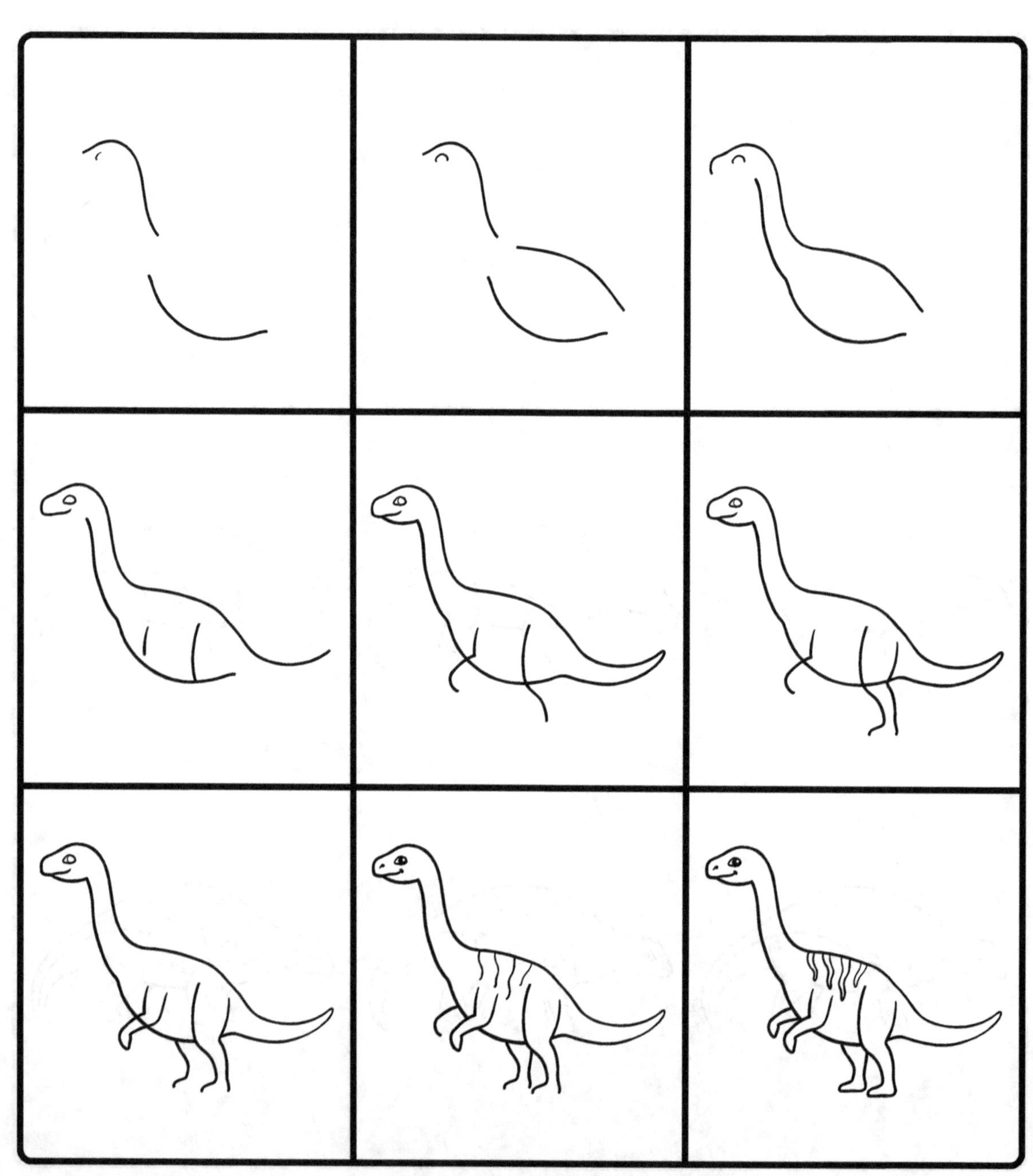

PSSITTACOSAURUS

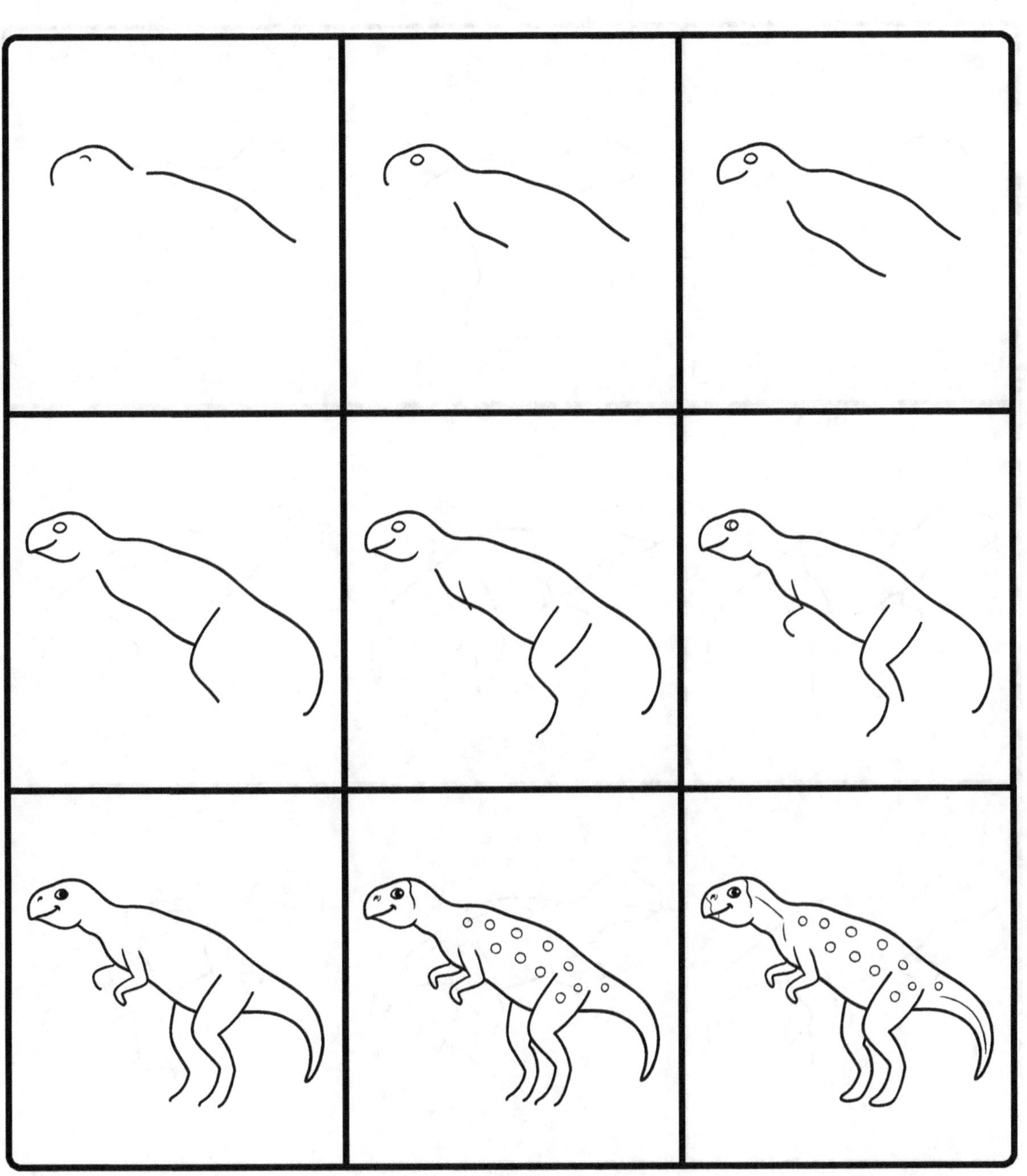

GIGANOTOSAURUS

ATTACKED BY SLICING WOUNDS.

50 FEET LONG – AS LONG AS A SPERM WHALE.

ARGENTINA

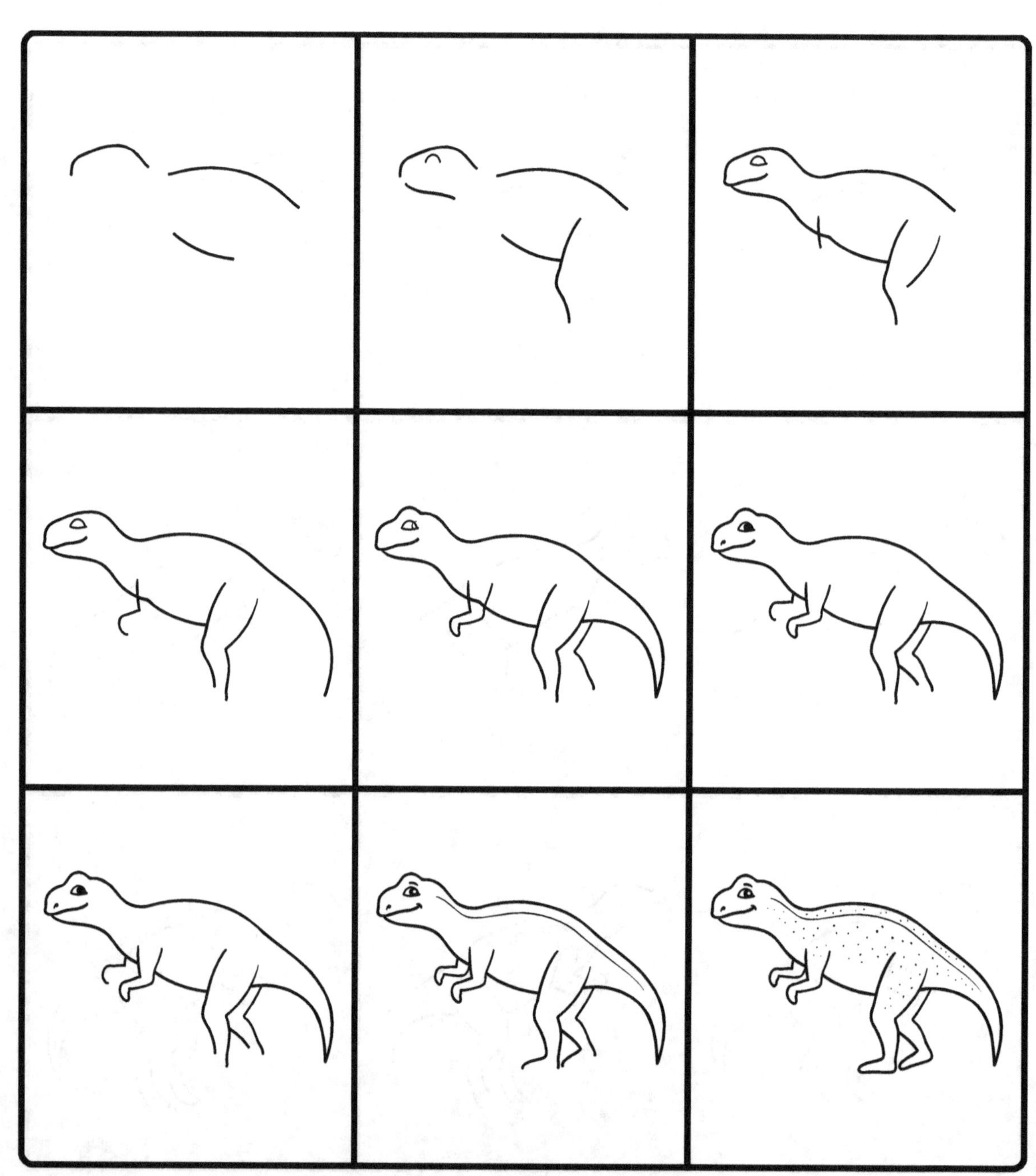

CENTROSAURUS

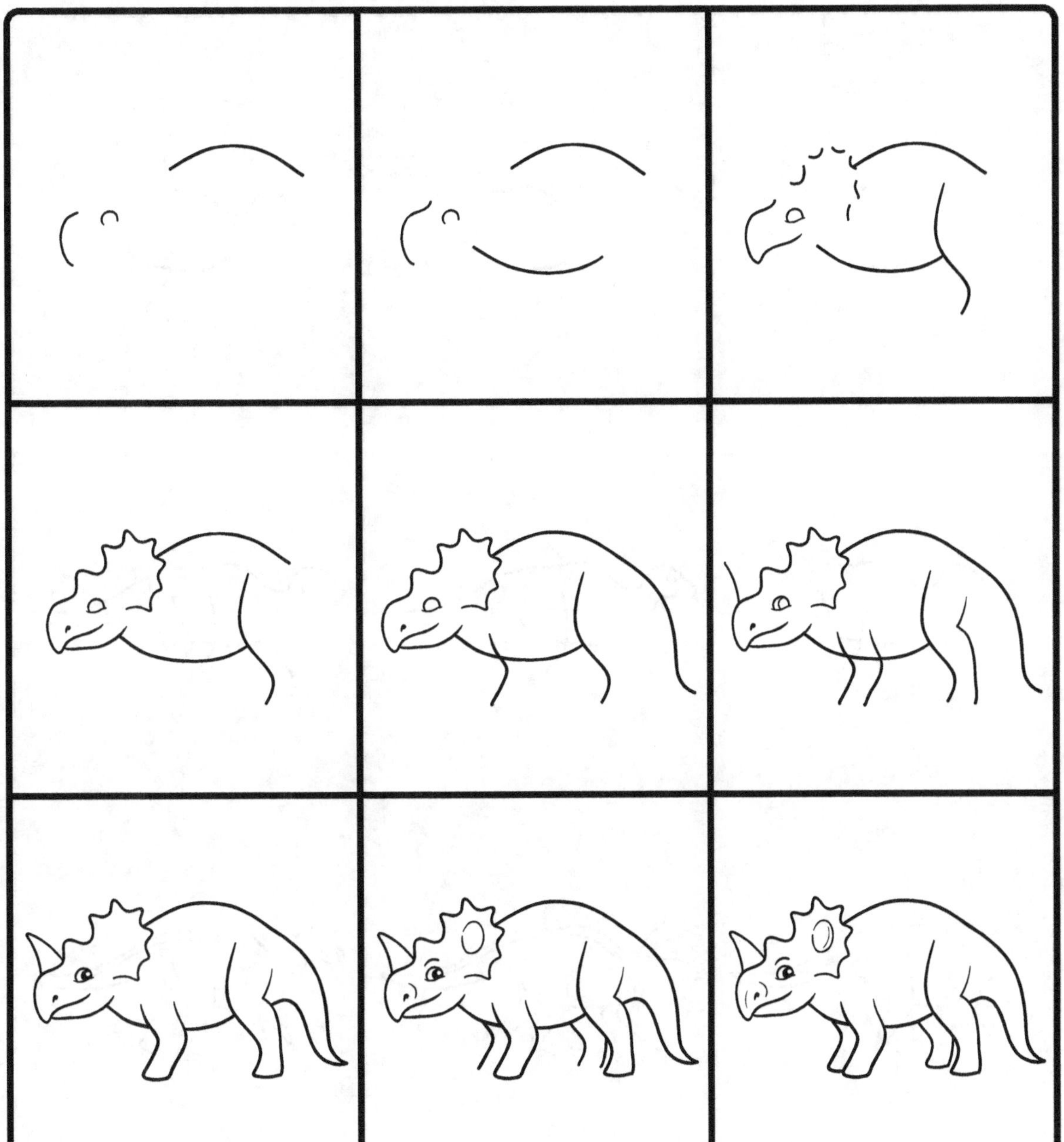

LAMBEOSAURUS

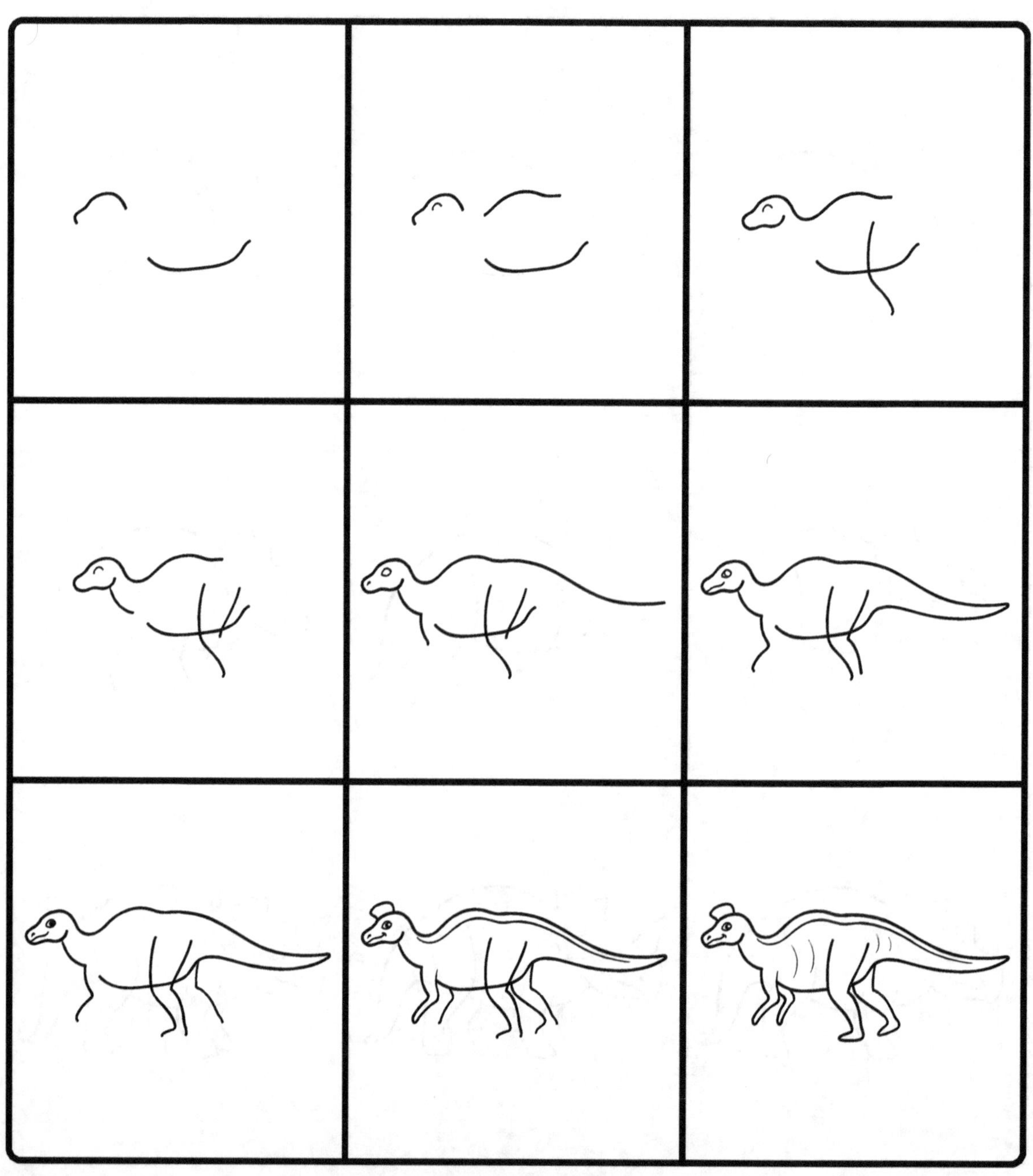

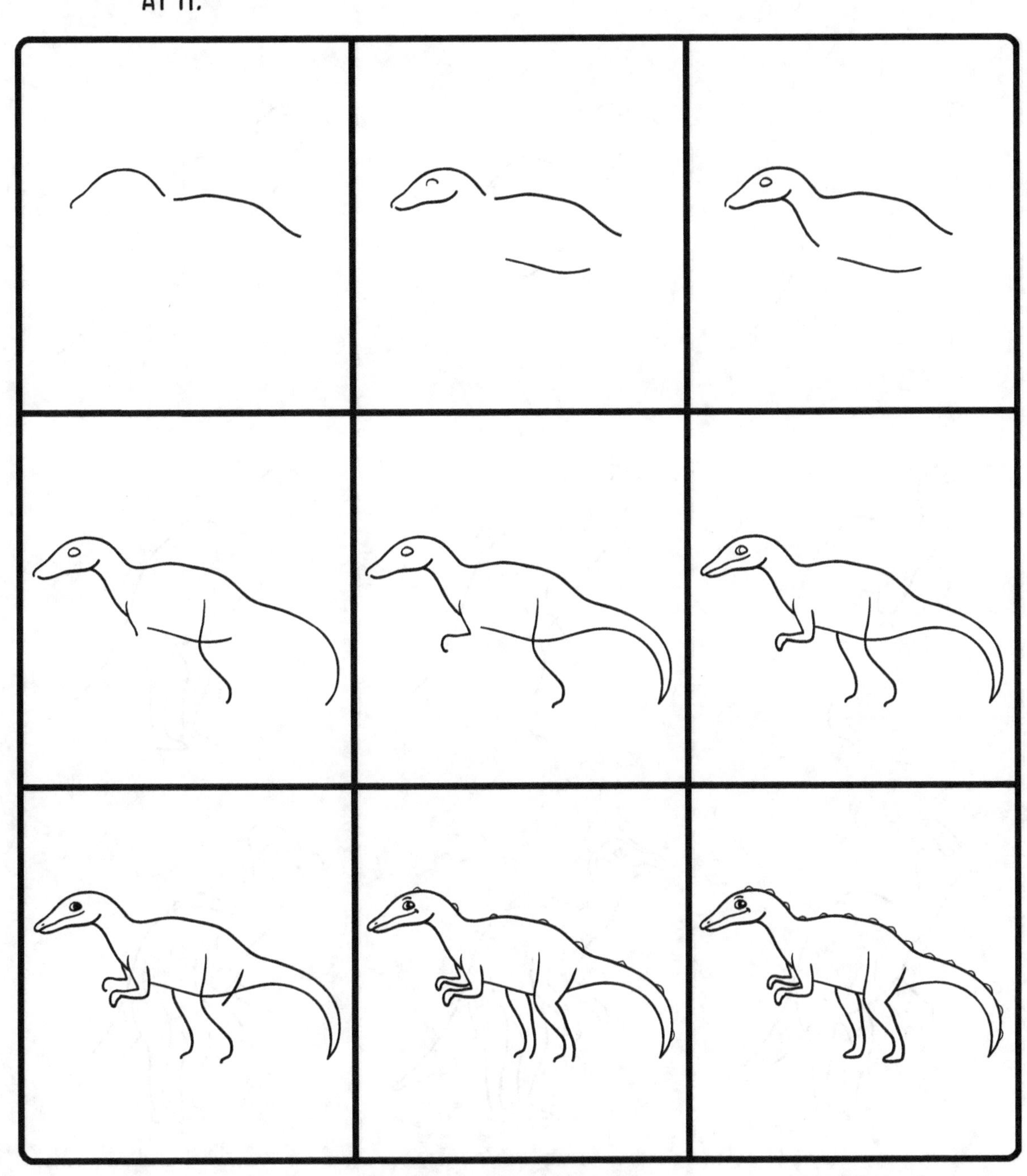

BARYONYX

FACT:
IS AN EXCELLENT SWIMMER AND WAITS FOR A HERBIVORE TO GET CLOSER BEFORE LUNGING AT IT.

SPEED:
15 MILES PER HOUR – AS FAST AS A TURKEY.

ORIGIN:
ENGLAND.

CORYTHOSAURUS

FACT:
LOVED TO EAT TWIGS!

SIZE:
7 FEET - A BIT TALLER
THAN A HORSE.

ORIGIN:
NORTH AMERICA.

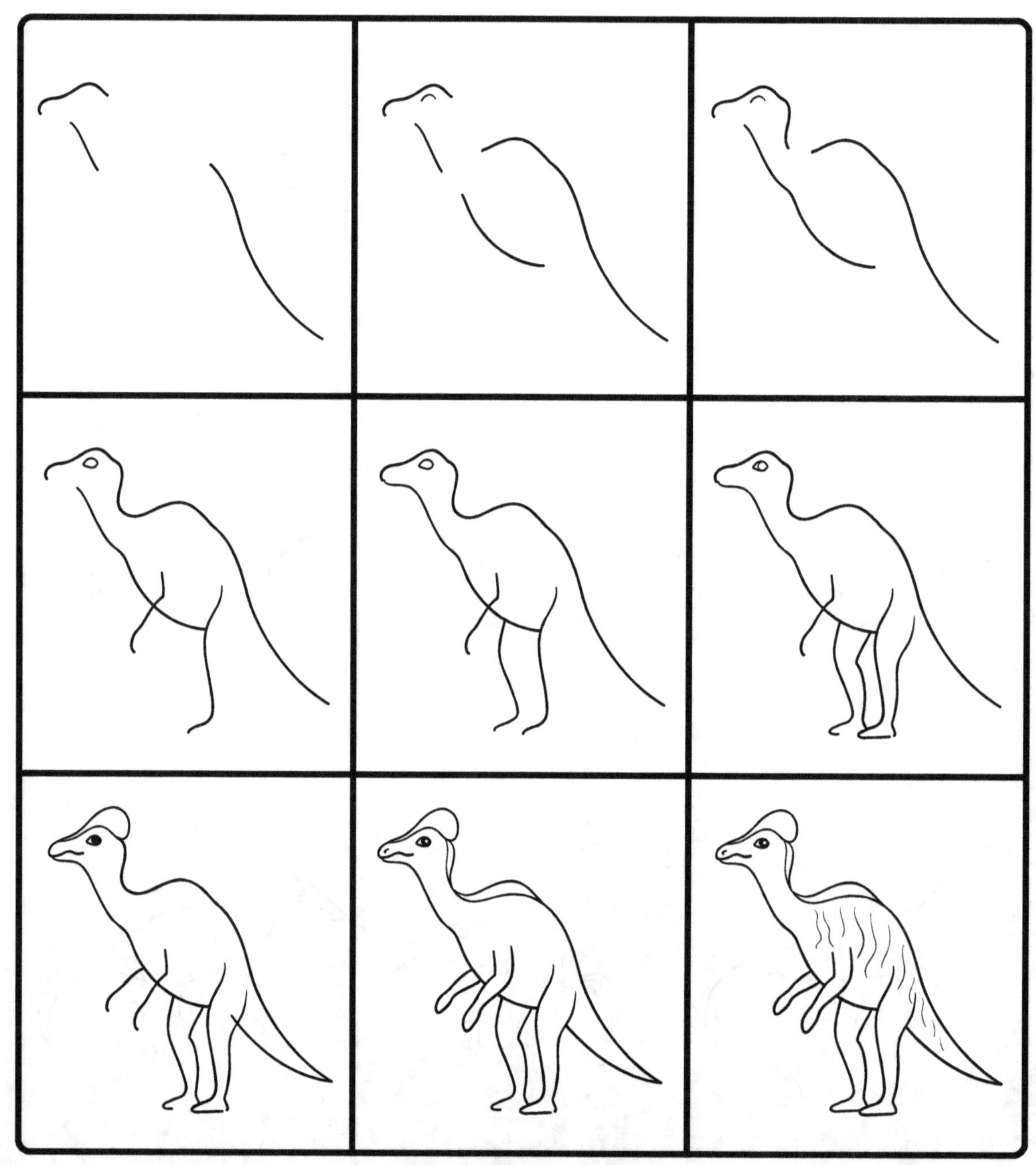

STYRACOSAURUS

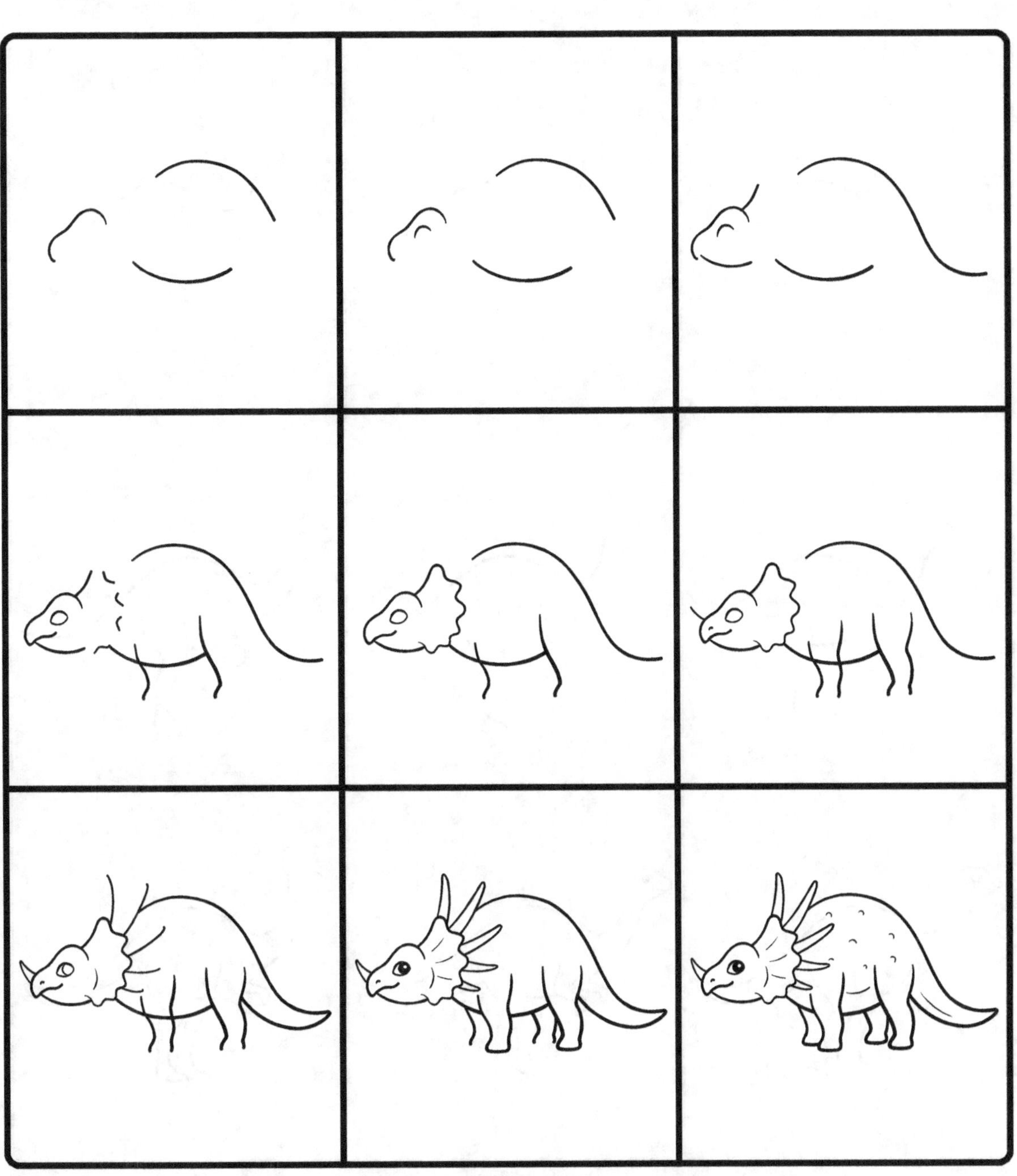

CALLIMIMUS

FACT:
WERE FAST ENOUGH TO OUTRUN MANY PREDATORS.

SPEED:
UP TO 35 MILES PER HOUR – AS FAST AS A HYENA.

ORIGIN:
MONGOLIA.

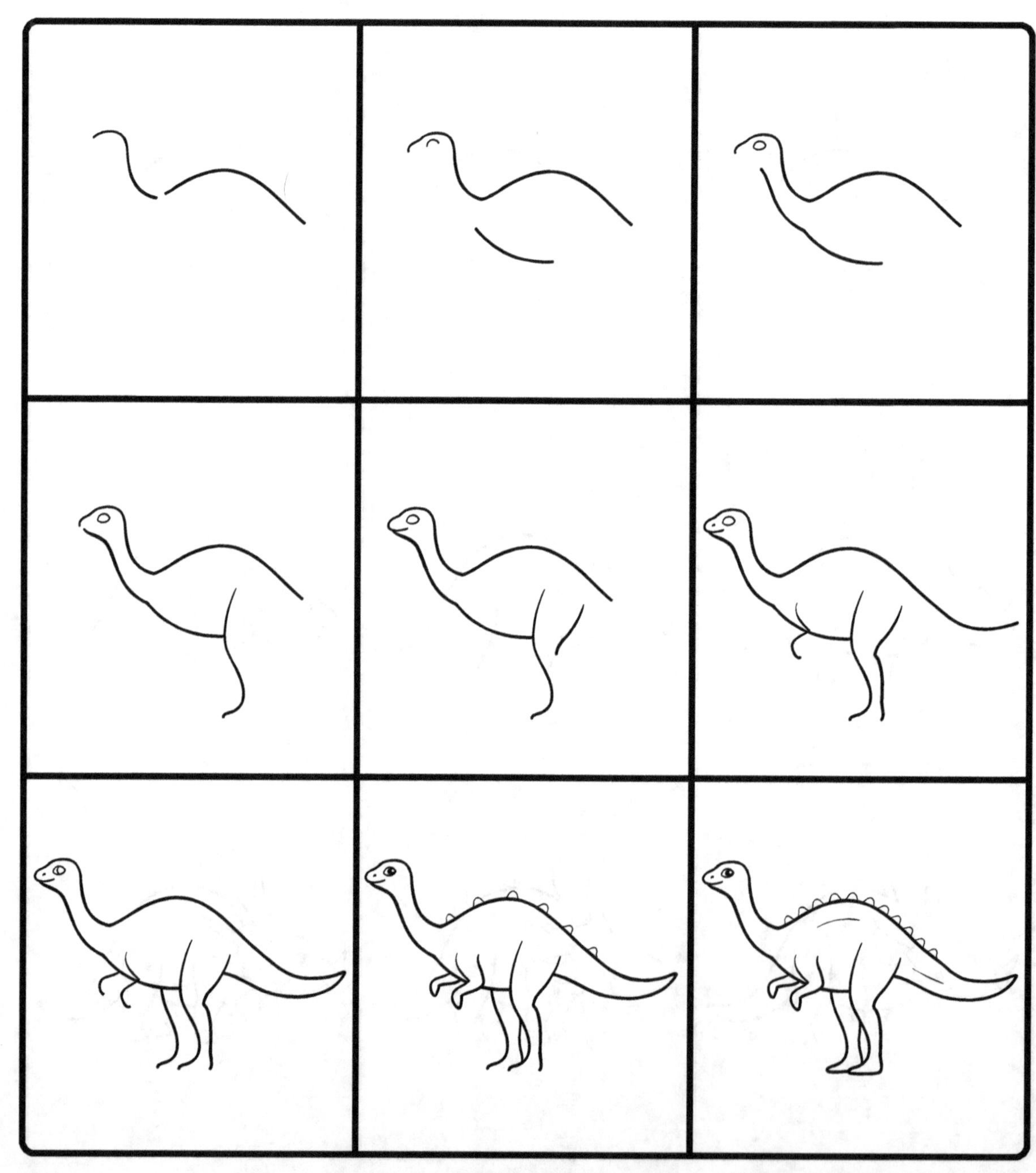

BRACHIOSAURUS

ITS LONG TAIL WOULD WHIP AWAY ATTACKERS!

30 FEET HIGH – AS TALL AS ONE AND A HALF GIRAFFES.

NORTH AMERICA.

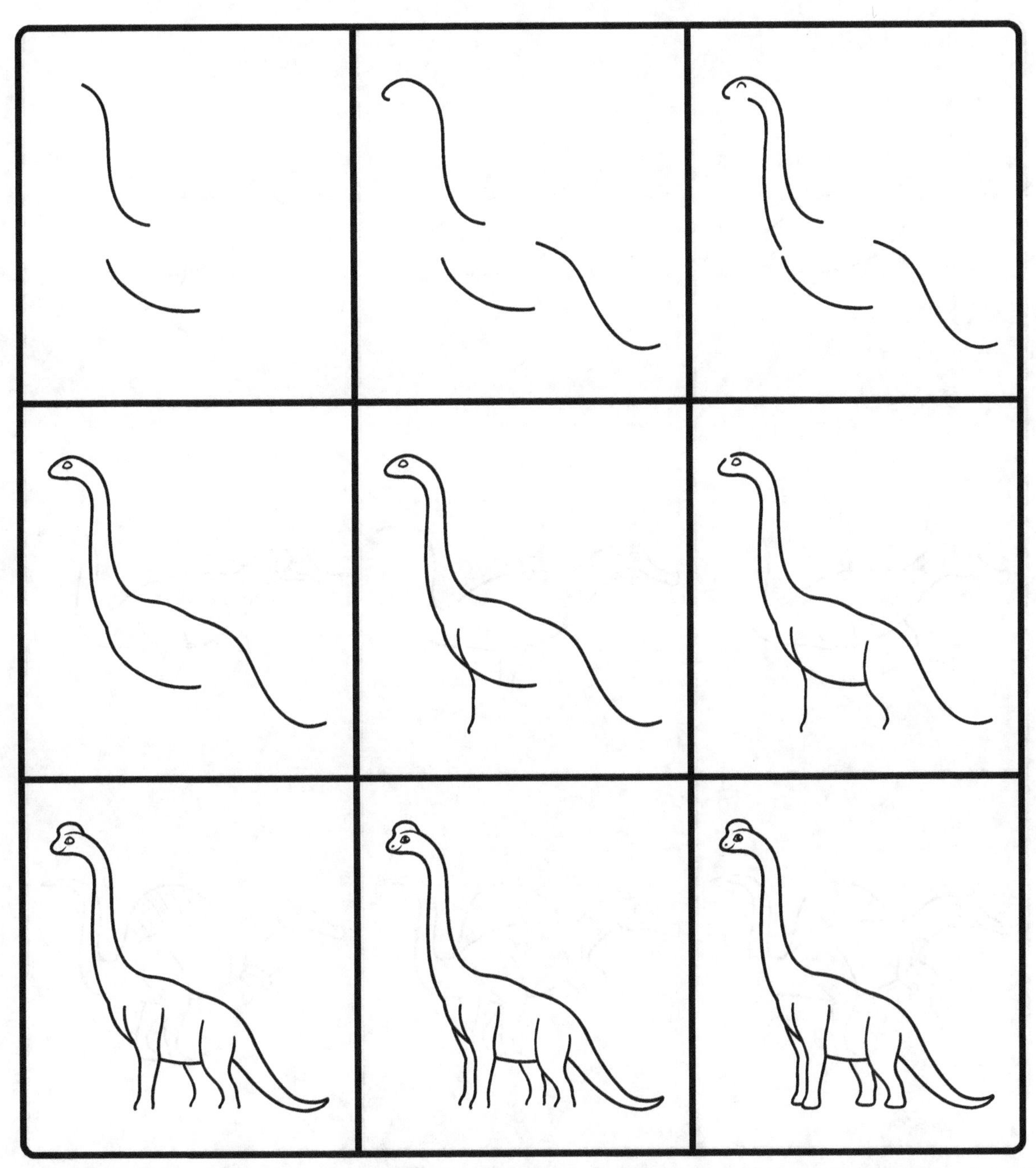

SPINOSAURUS

HUNTED FISH, AND ALSO ATTACKED ANYTHING THAT COMES NEAR THE WATER WITH ITS CLAWS AND TEETH.

15 MILES PER HOUR - AS FAST AS A BROWN BEAR.

NORTH AFRICA.

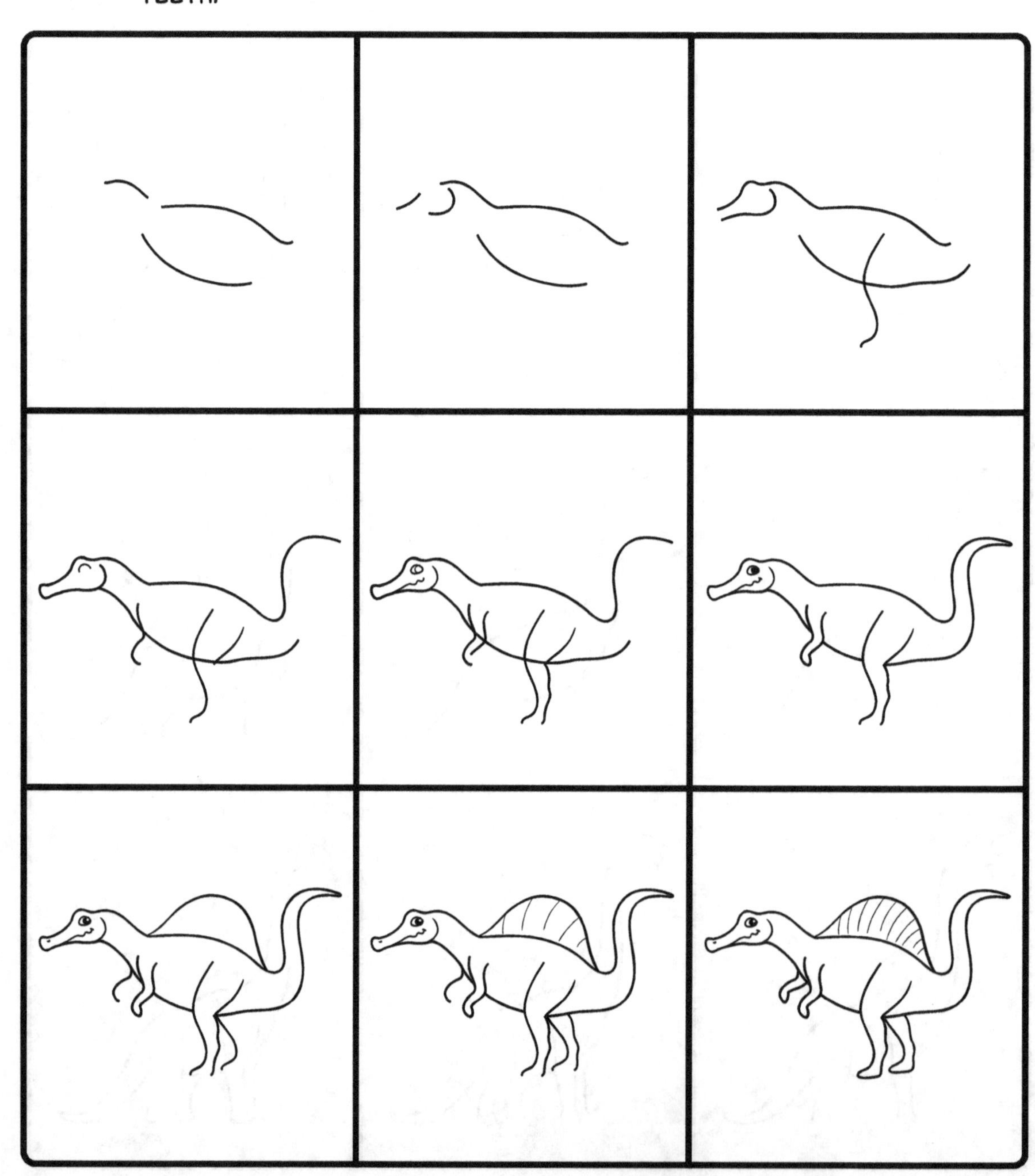

CERATOSAURUS

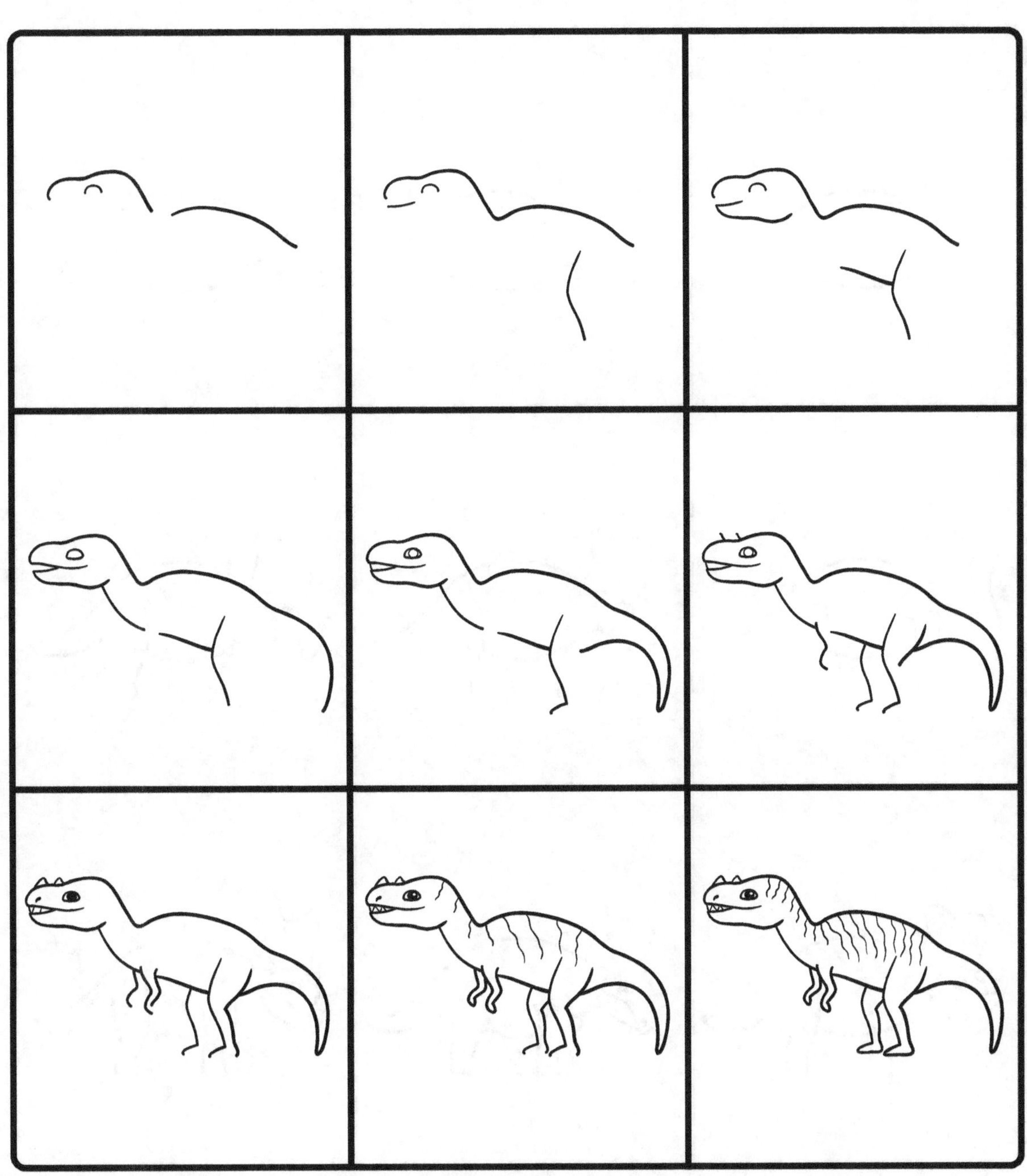

CHASMOSAURUS

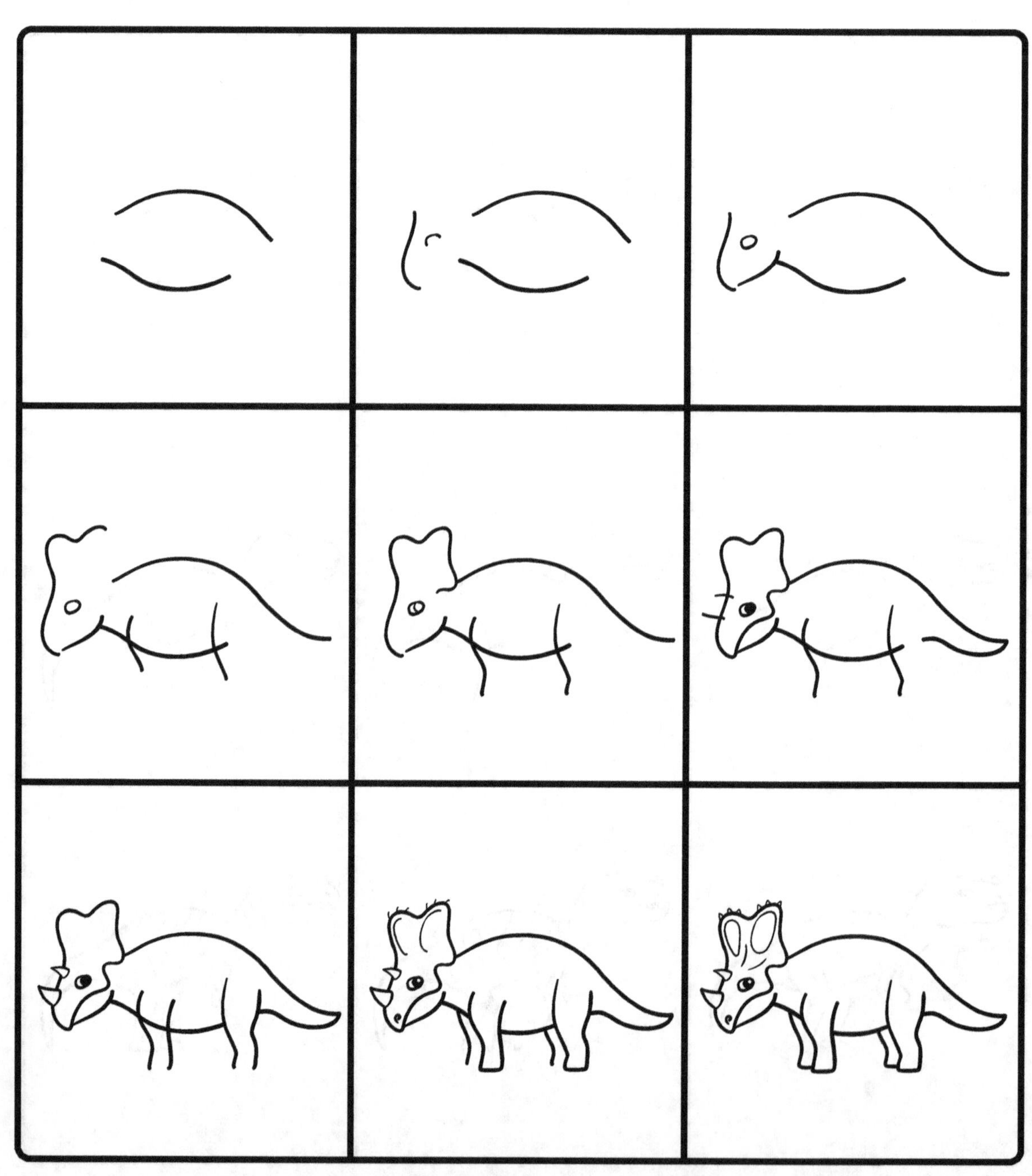

ACANTHOPHOLIS

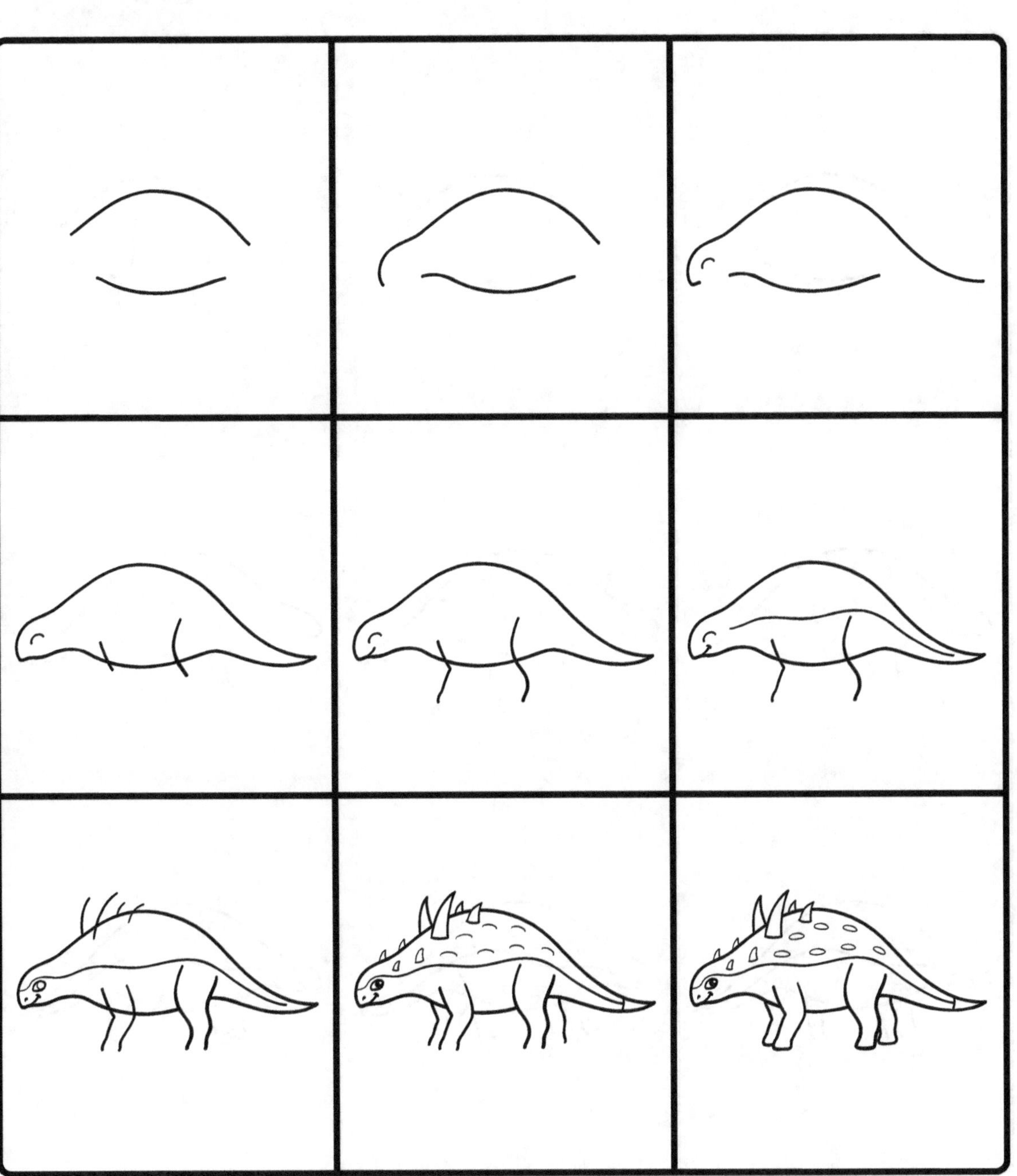

NODOSAURUS

FACT:
HAD SOME ARMOR FOR PROTECTION BUT MOST LIKELY HID FROM PREDATORS.

SIZE:
10 FEET – AS TALL AS AN OSTRICH.

ORIGIN:
NORTH AMERICA.

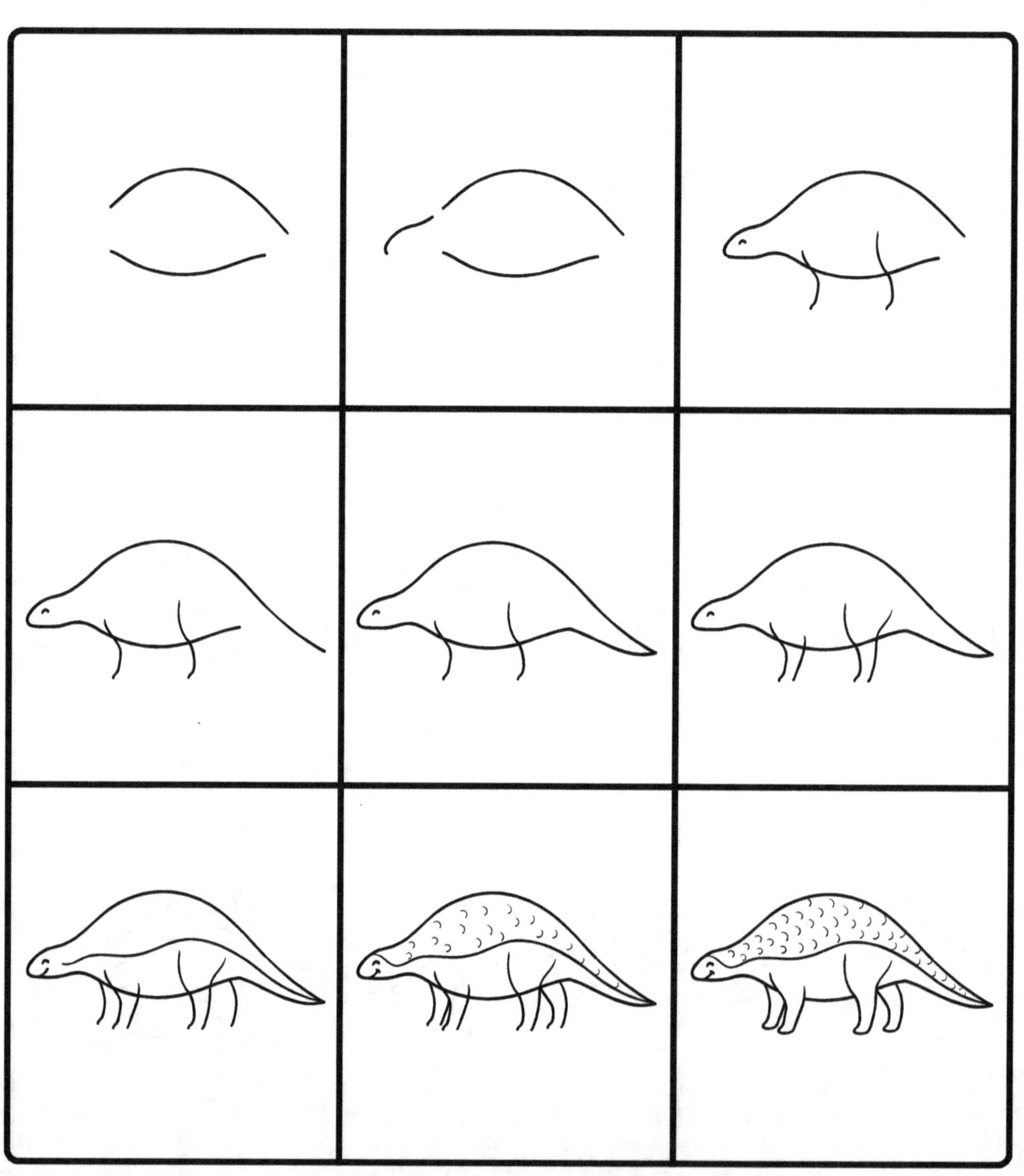

OURANOSAURUS

THEY WOULD HAVE BEEN EASY PREY WITH FEW DEFENSES.

11 FEET – AS BIG AS A SMALL ELEPHANT.

AFRICA.

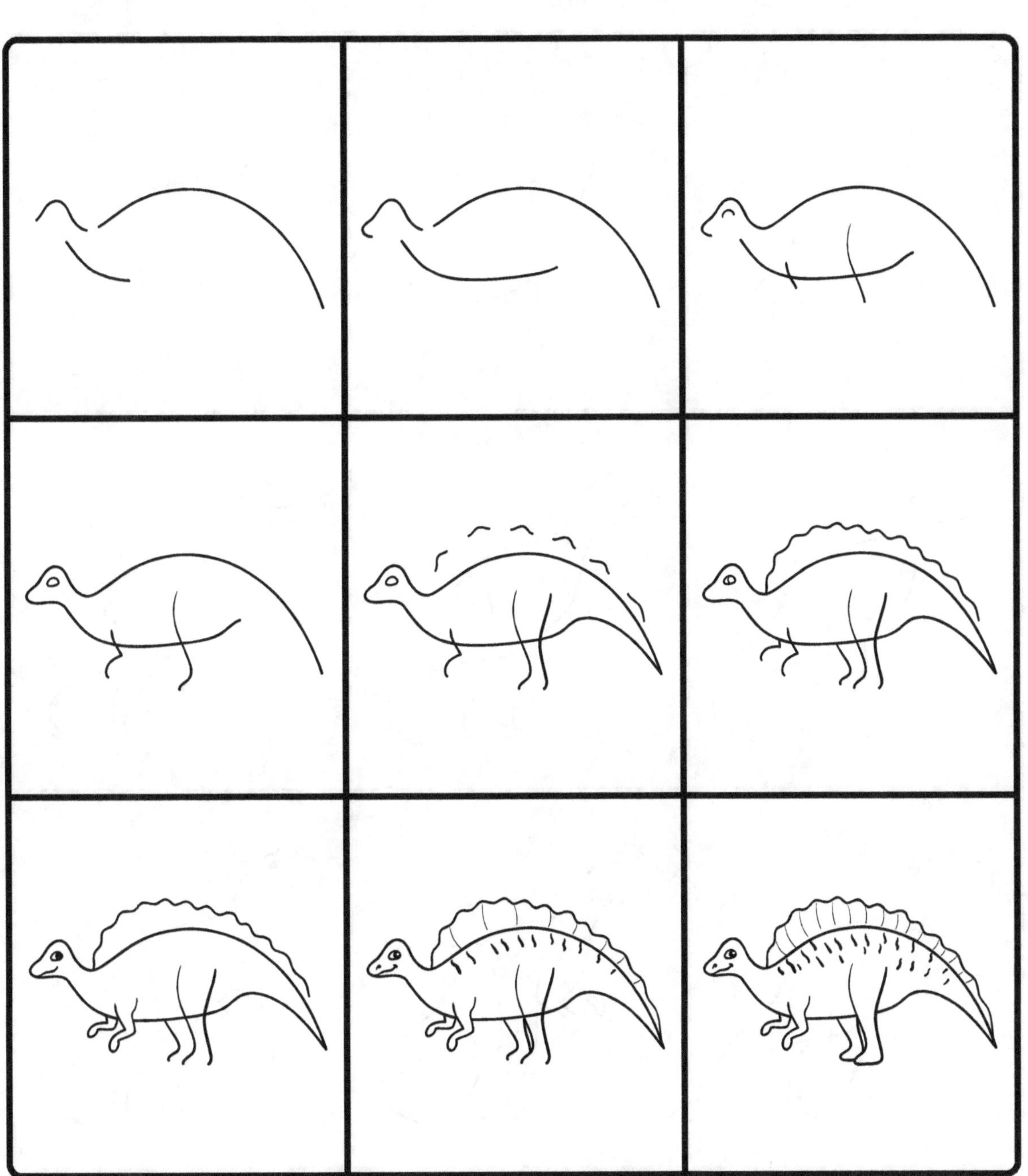

ALLOSAURUS

FACT:
IT ATTACKED BY USING ITS SKULL AS A HATCHET AND BITING AND SLASHING WITH ITS TEETH.

SIZE:
16.5 FEET - ABOUT AS TALL AS 3 ADULTS.

ORIGIN:
UTAH.

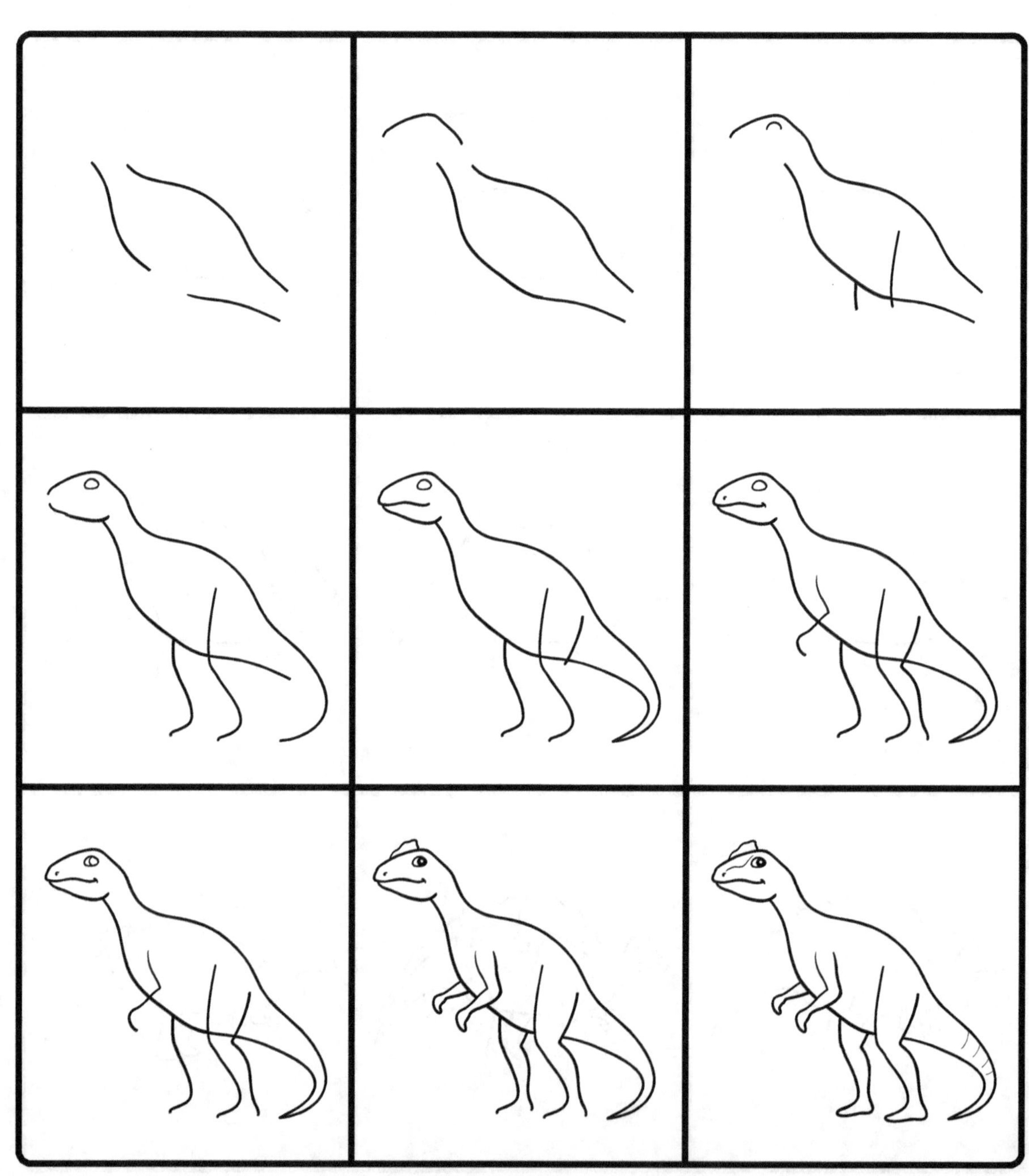

DICRAEOSAURUS

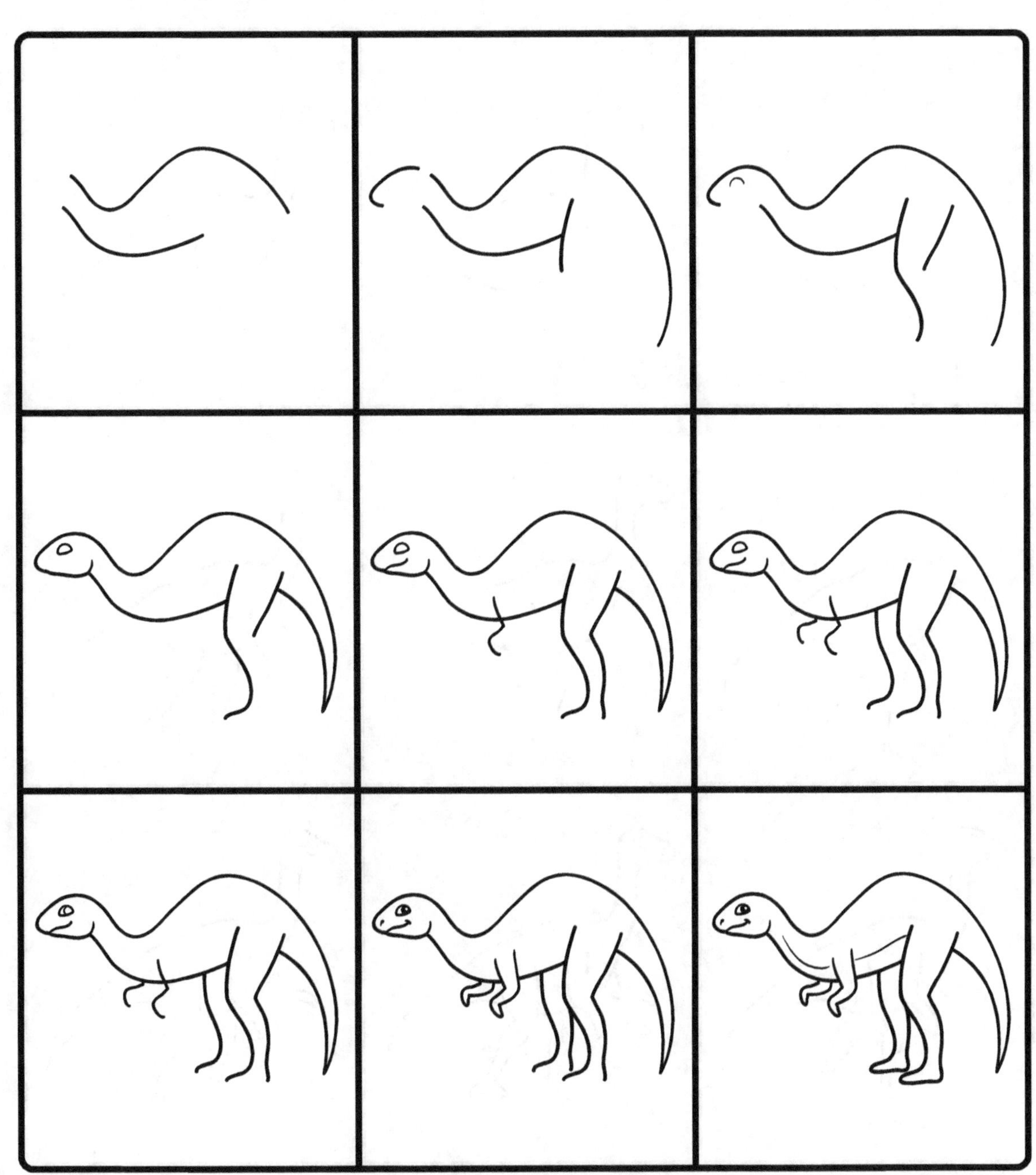

TROODON

FACT:
HAS A VENOMOUS BITE!

SPEED:
37 MILES PER HOUR – AS
FAST AS A WILDEBEEST.

ORIGIN:
MONTANA.

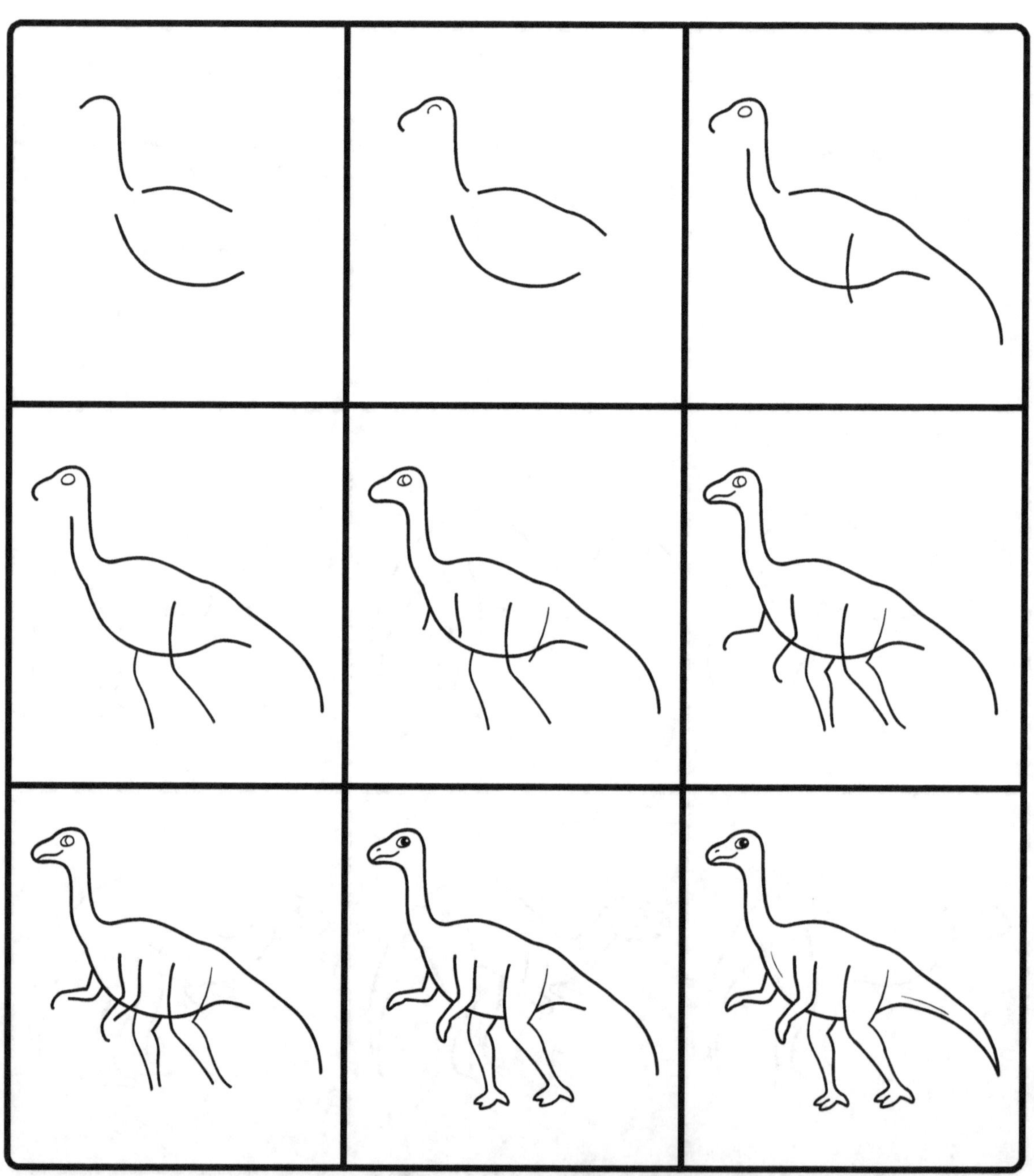

ULTRASAURUS

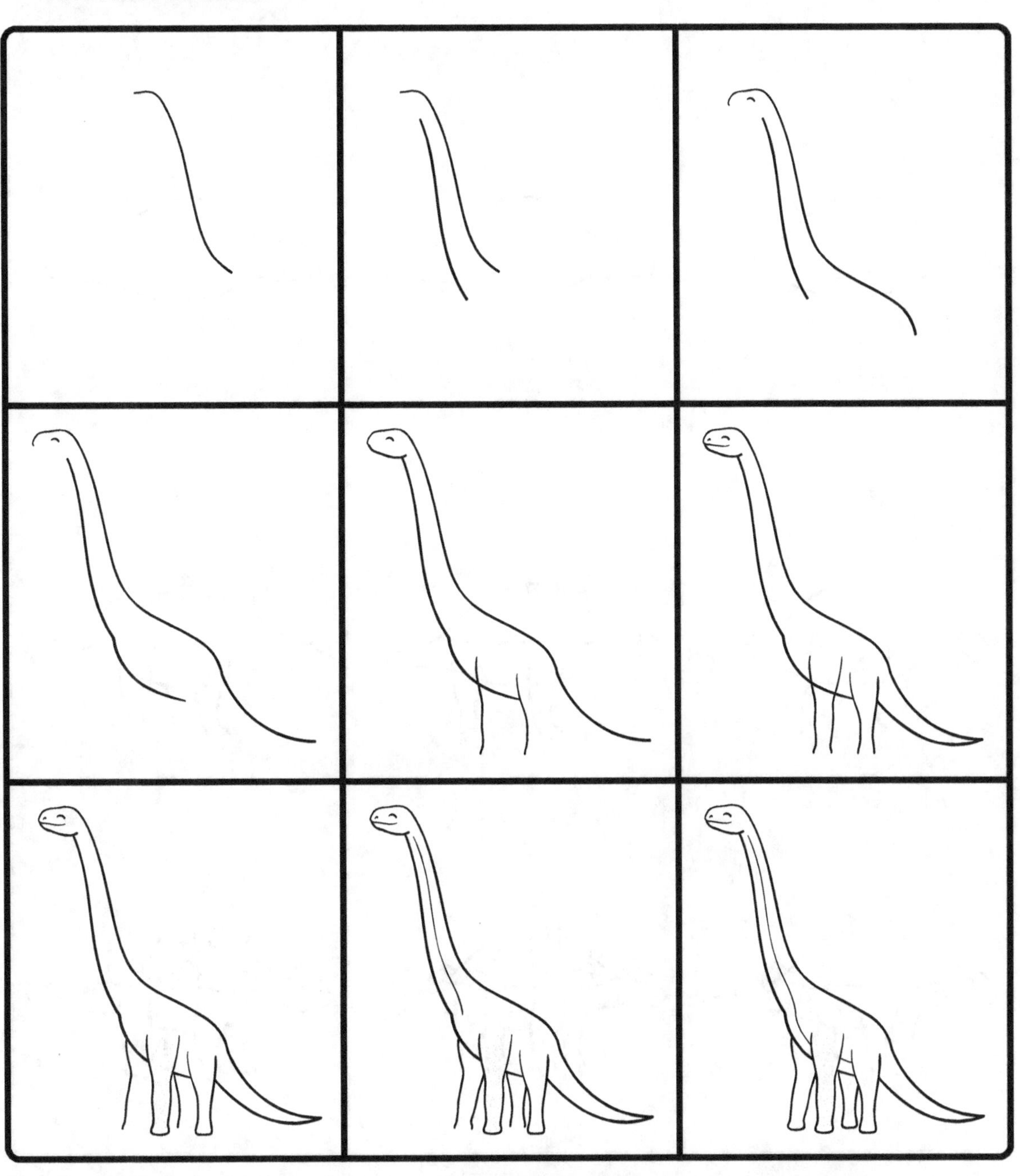

ANKYLOSAURUS

FACT:

IT HAS VERY THICK ARMOR THAT JOINED UP TO A CLUB ON ITS TAIL THAT IT CAN USE TO SWING AT PREDATORS!

SIZE:

5.5 FEET – AS TALL AS A HIPPO.

ORIGIN:

NORTH AMERICA.

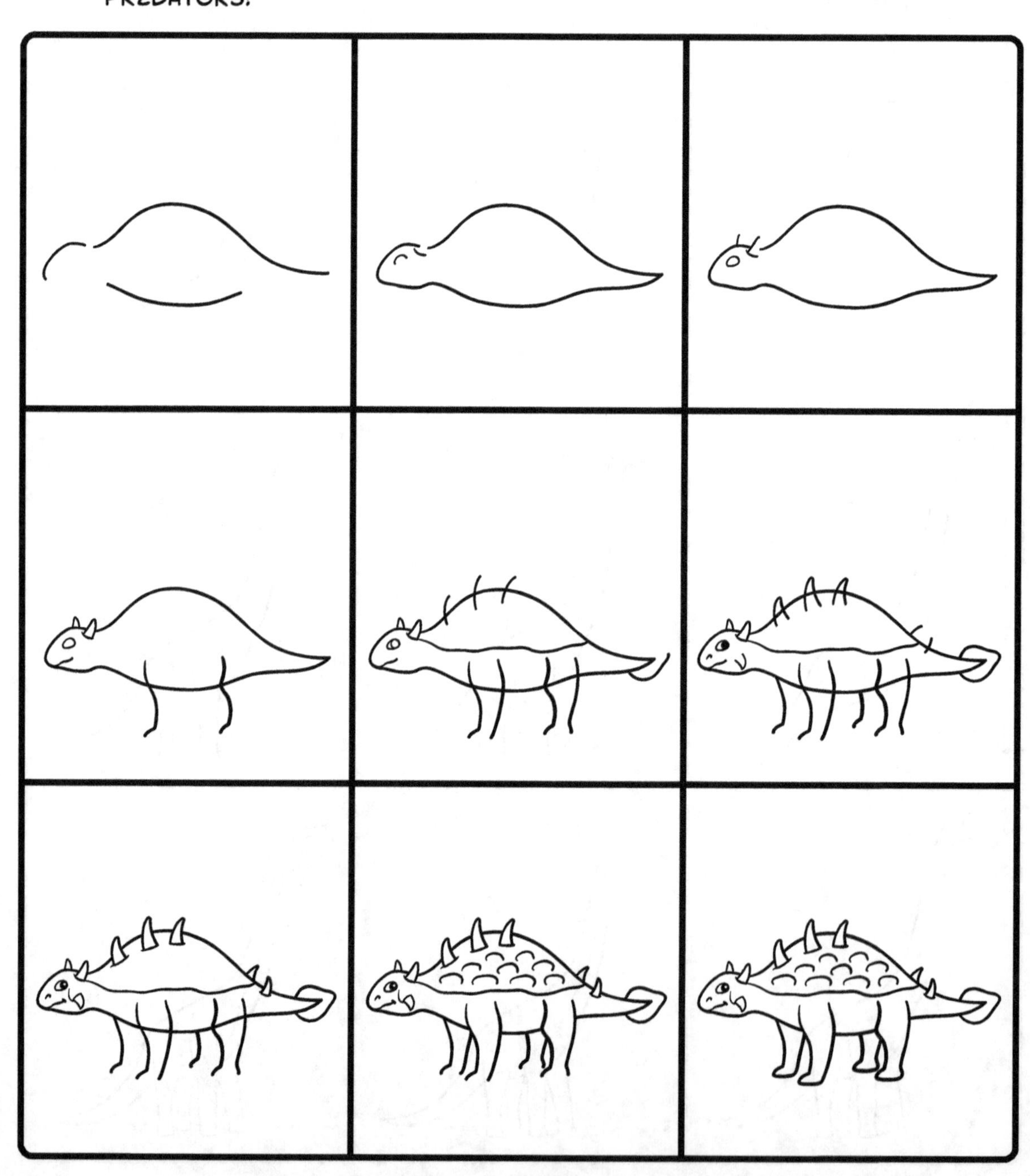

UTAHRAPTOR

FACT:
HUNTED ITS PREY WITH ITS SICKLE-SHAPED CLAWS.

SIZE:
6 FEET - AS TALL AS A HORSE.

ORIGIN:
NORTH AMERICA.

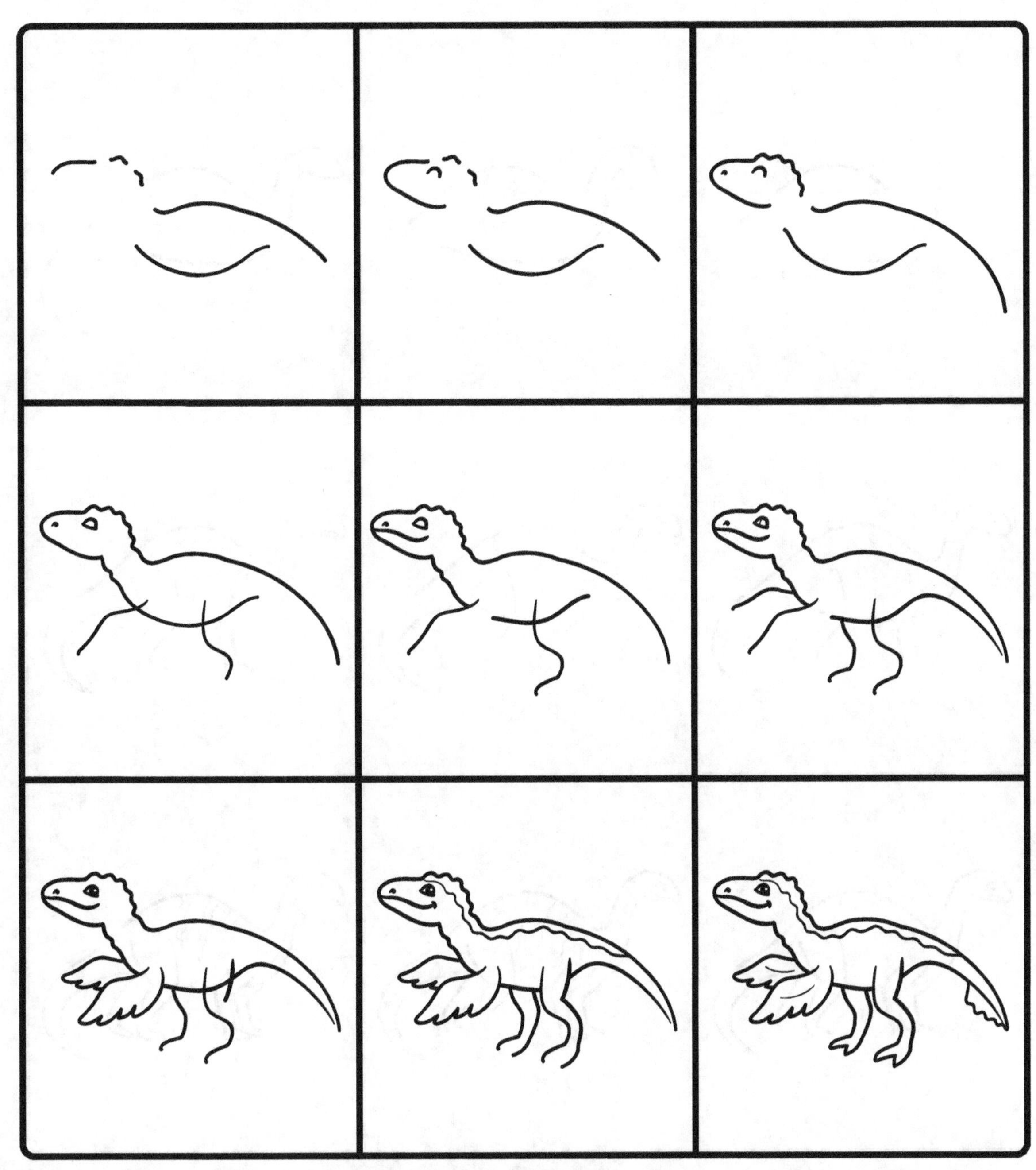

THECODONTOSAURUS

FACT:
IT RUNS FAST TO ESCAPE PREDATORS.

SIZE:
ONE FOOT – AS TALL AS AN ANTEATER.

ORIGIN:
SOUTH ENGLAND.

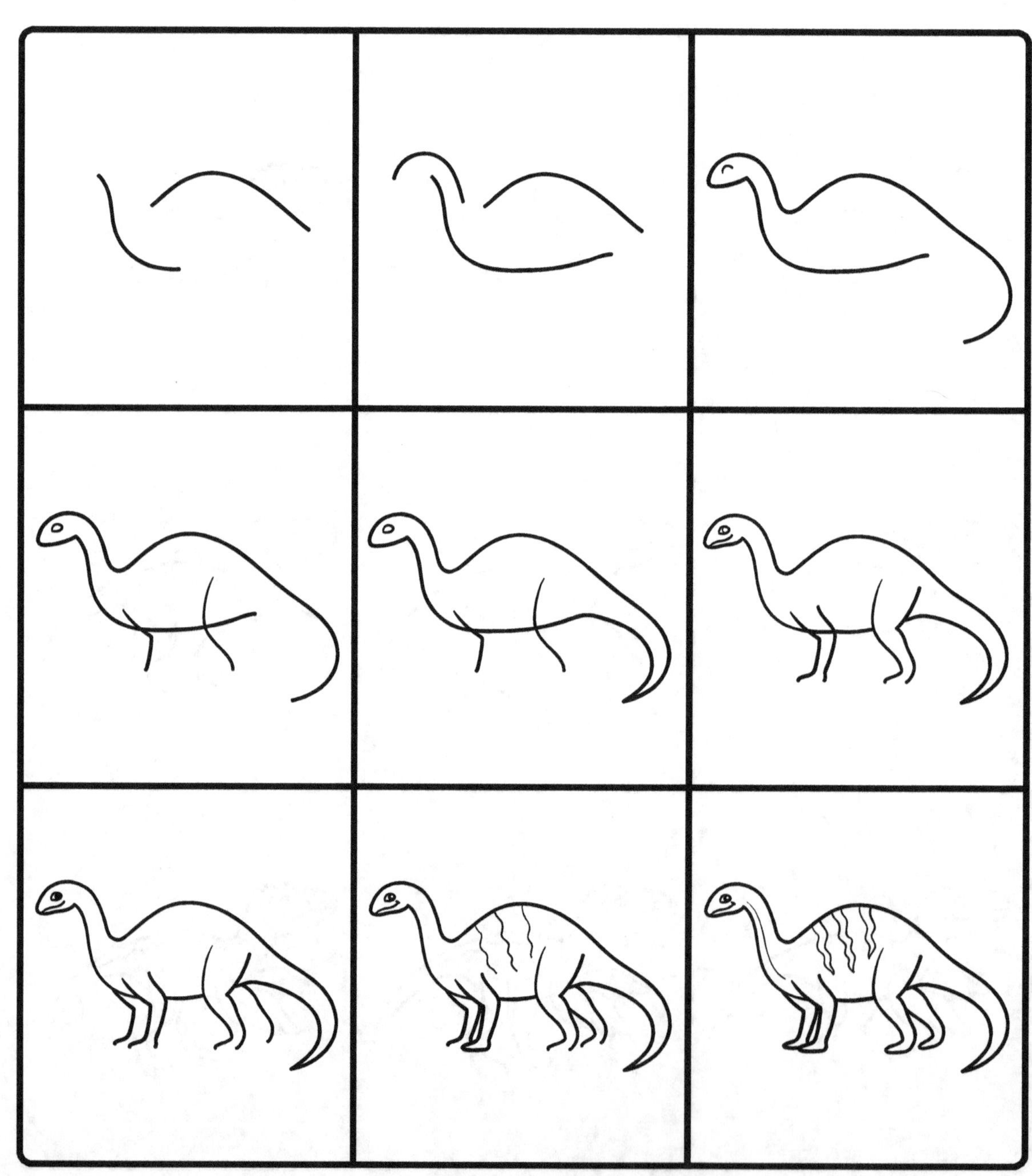

VELOCIRAPTOR

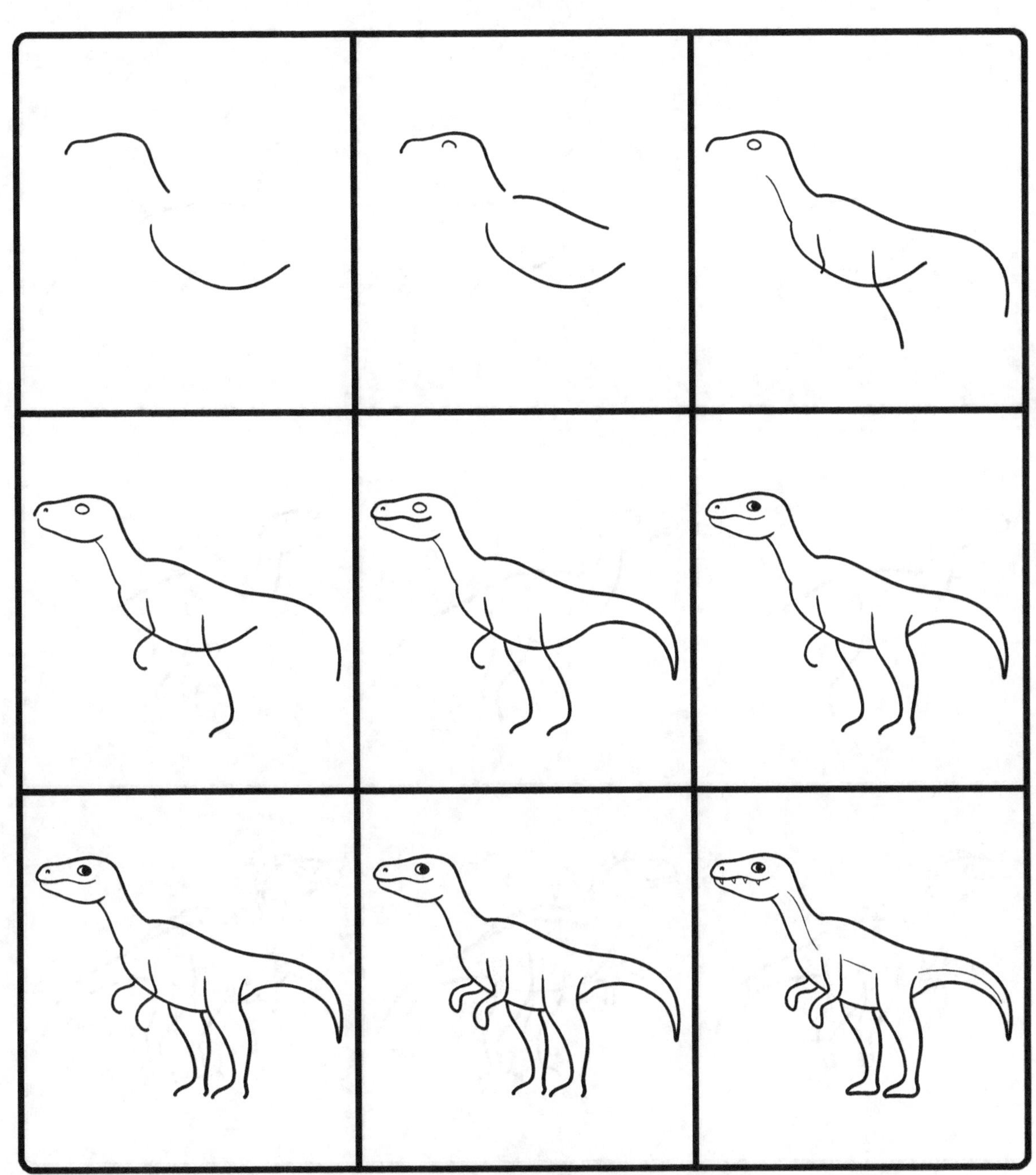

DEINONYCHUS

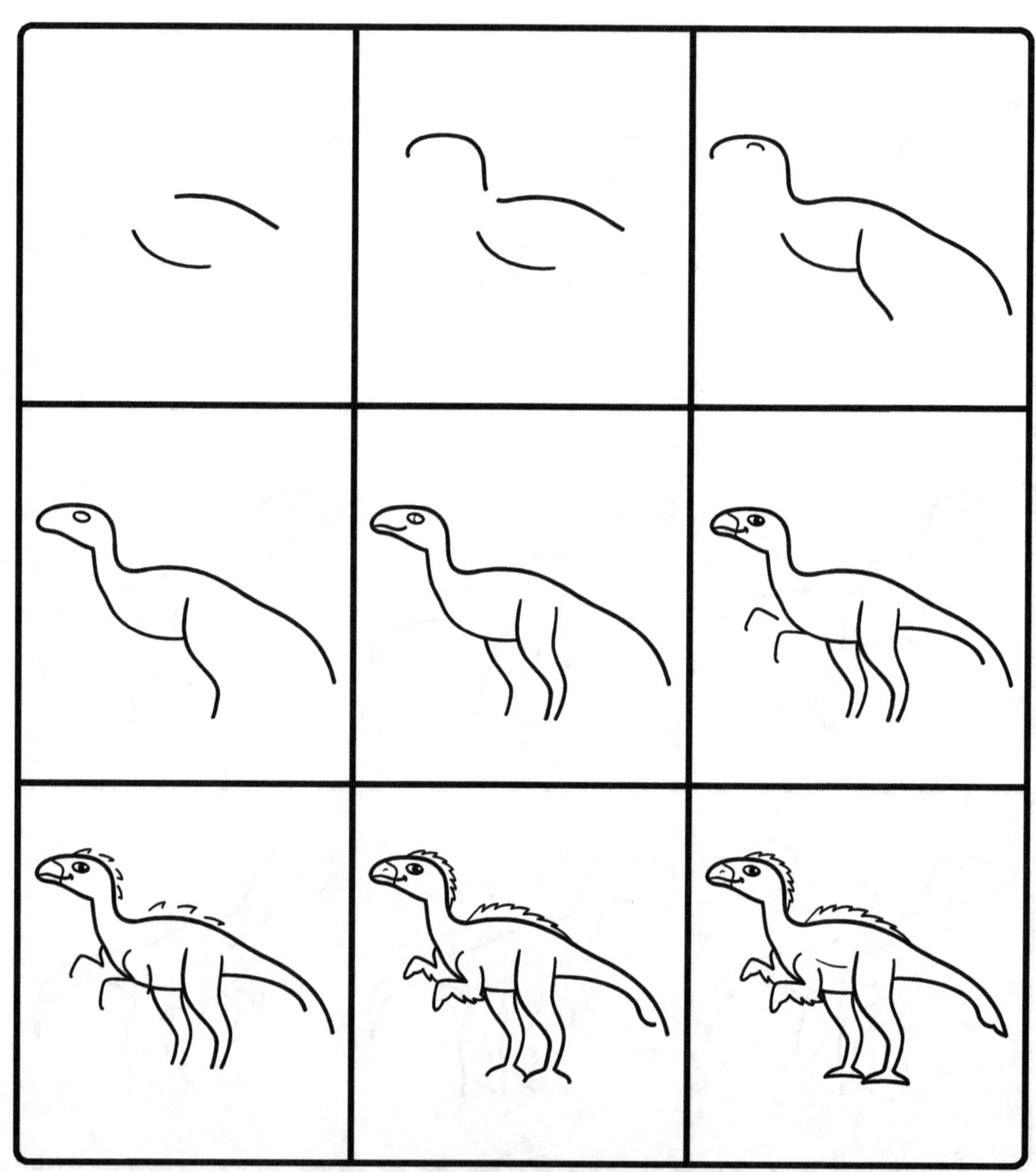

APATOSAURUS

USES ITS LONG TAIL TO WHIP PREDATORS, WARNING THEM TO BACK OFF.

80 FEET - AS LONG AS A BLUE WHALE.

NORTH AMERICA.

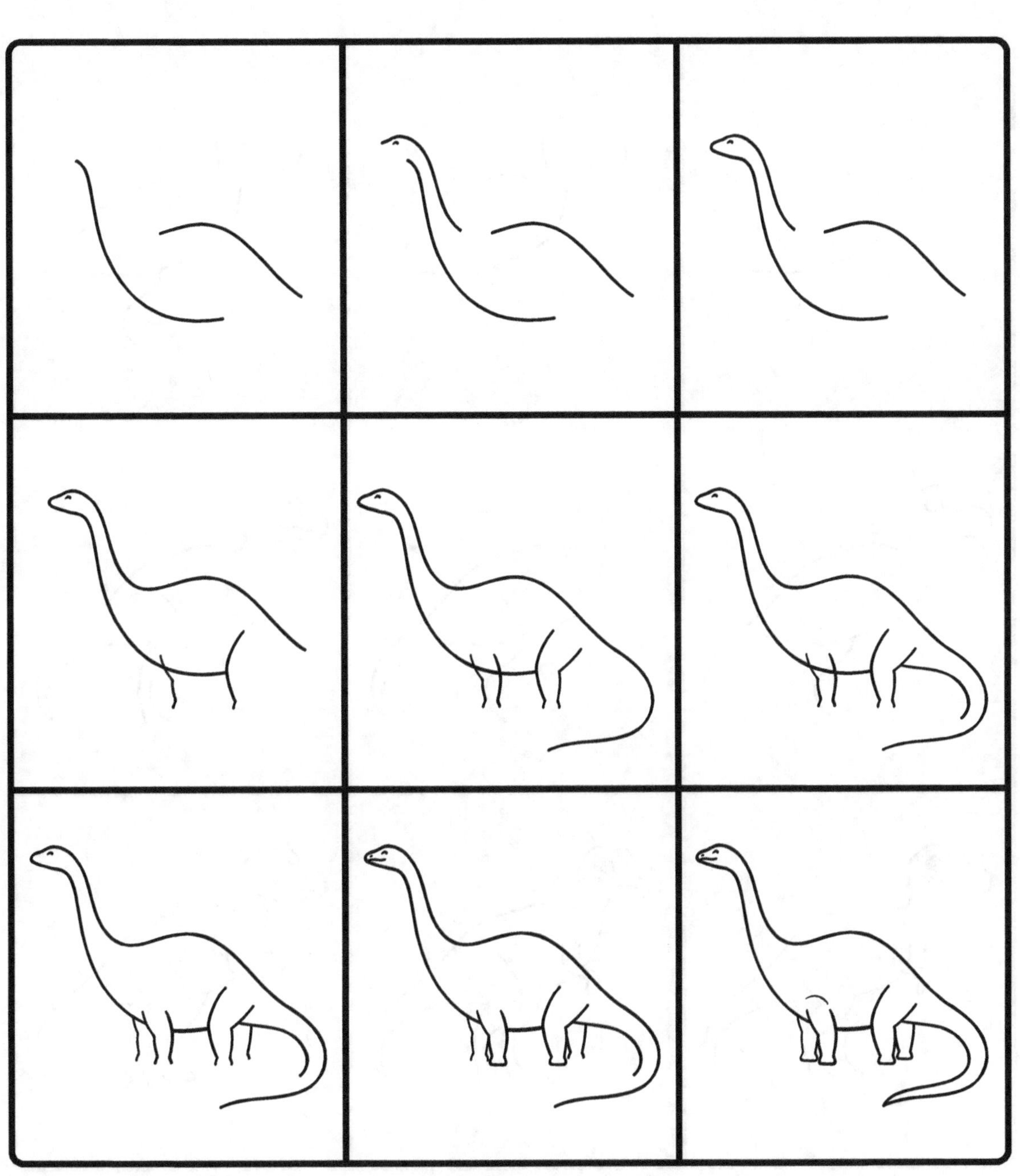

ALBERTOSAURUS

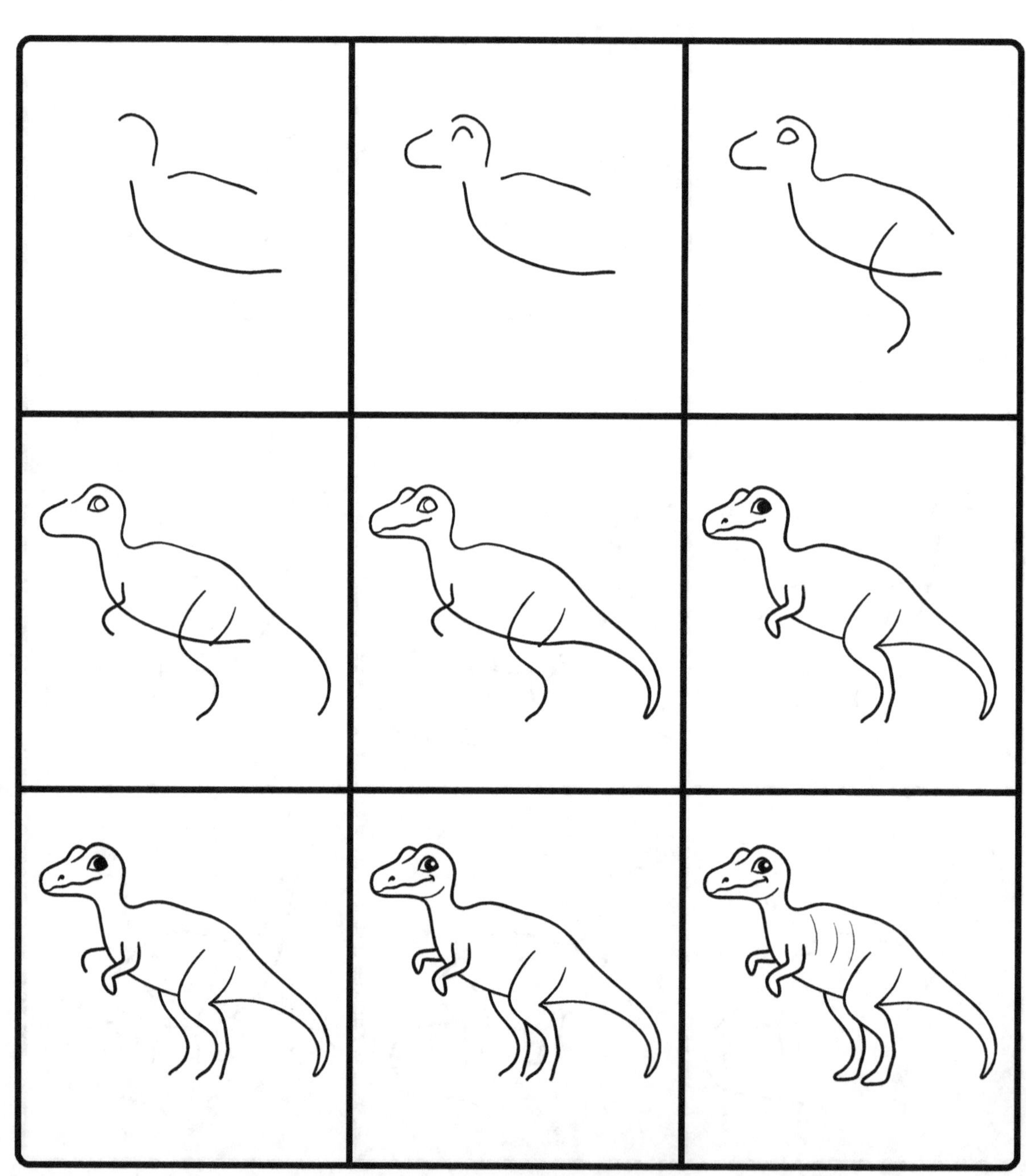

PTERANODON

FACT:

HUNTS WITH ITS LONG BEAK, CATCHING SMALL PREY LIKE FISH.

SIZE:

WORLD'S BIGGEST FLYING REPTILE - WITH A WINGSPAN AS WIDE AS 7 METERS.

ORIGIN:

NORTH AMERICA.

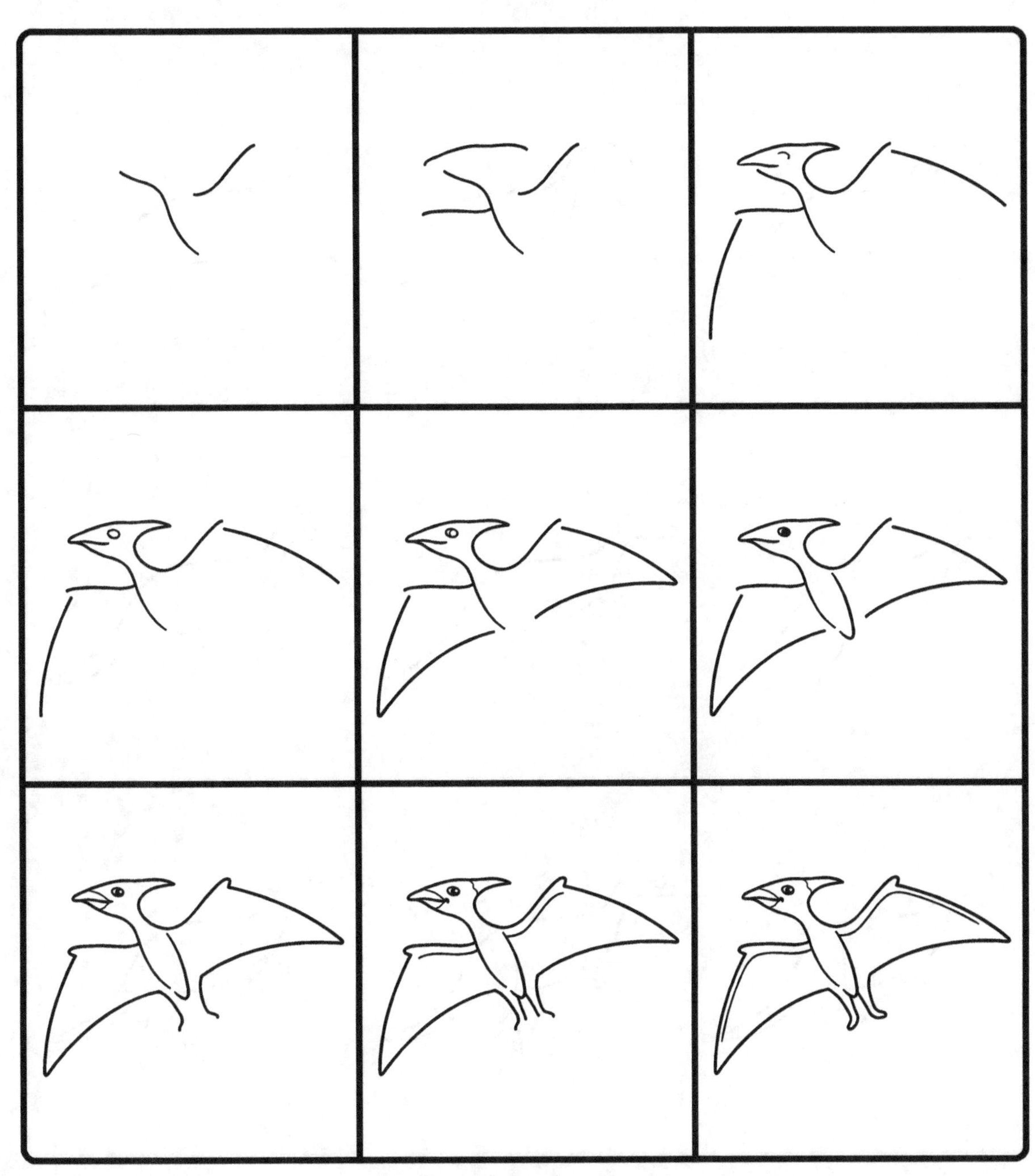

DRYOSAURUS

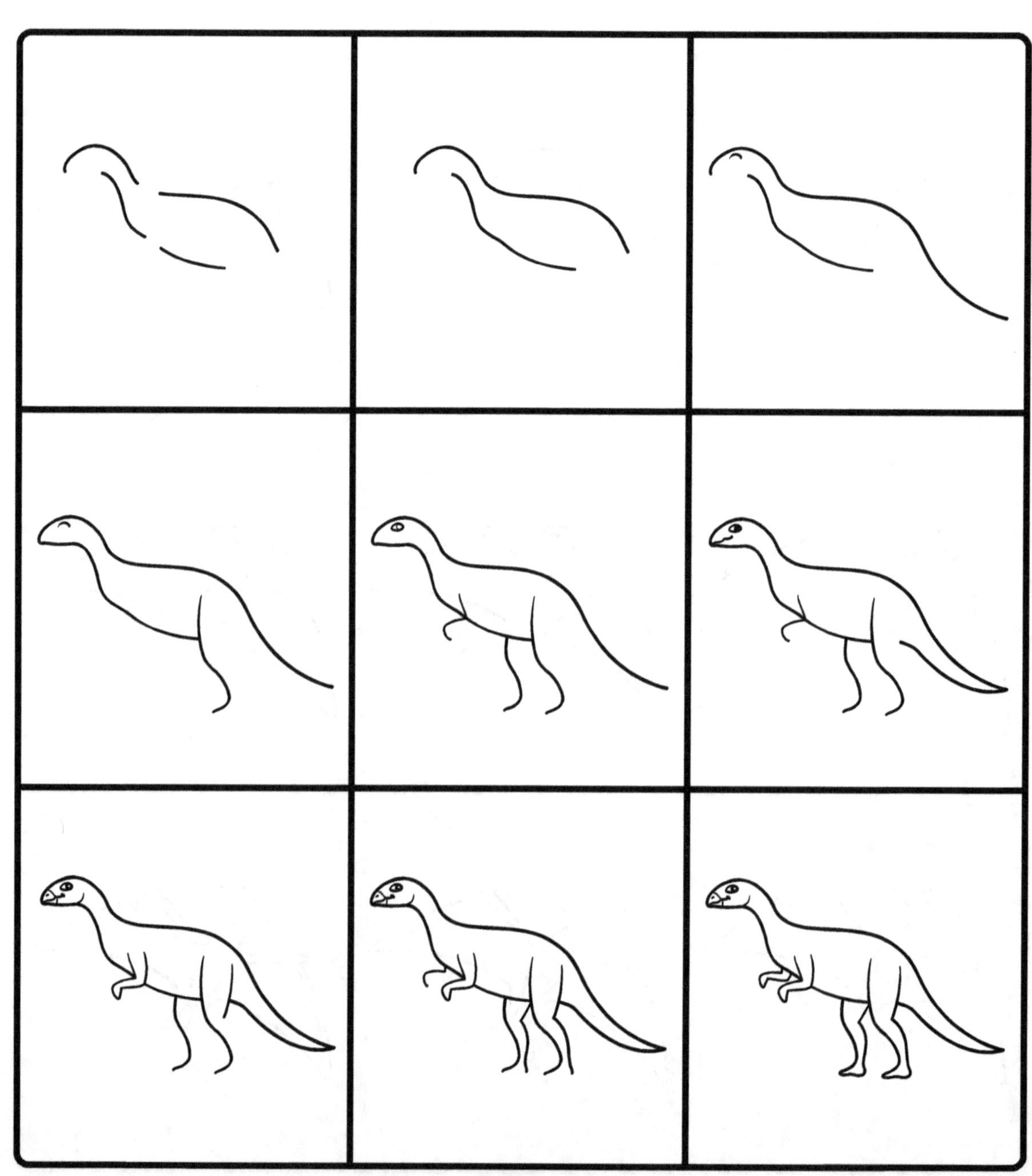

FACT:
FAST ENOUGH TO OUTRUN PREDATORS, OTHERWISE HIDES IN ITS BURROW.

SPEED:
31 MILES PER HOUR - AS FAST AS A RACING RABBIT.

ORIGIN:
NORTH AMERICA AND AFRICA.

COELOPHYSIS

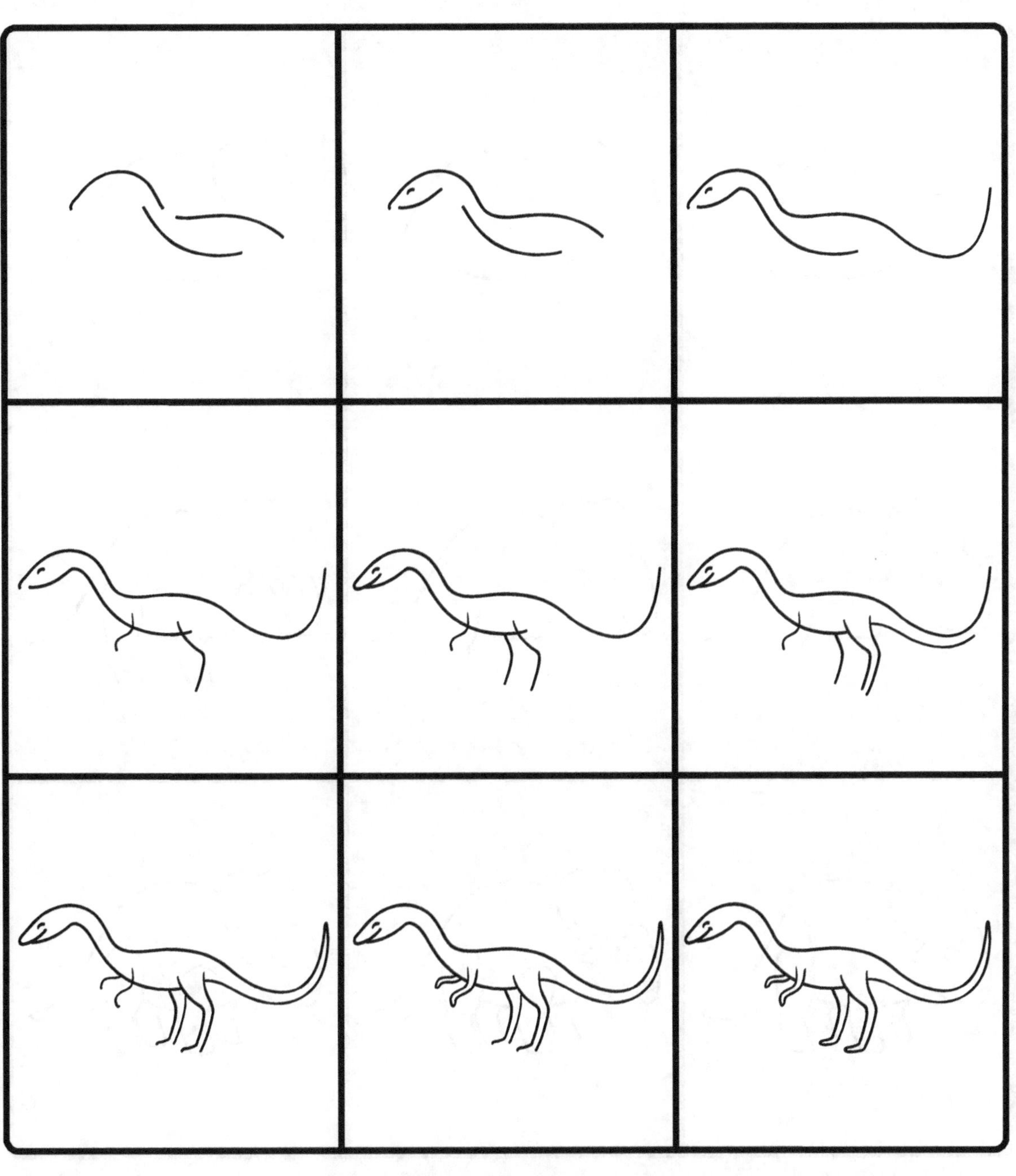

PACHYRHINOSAURUS

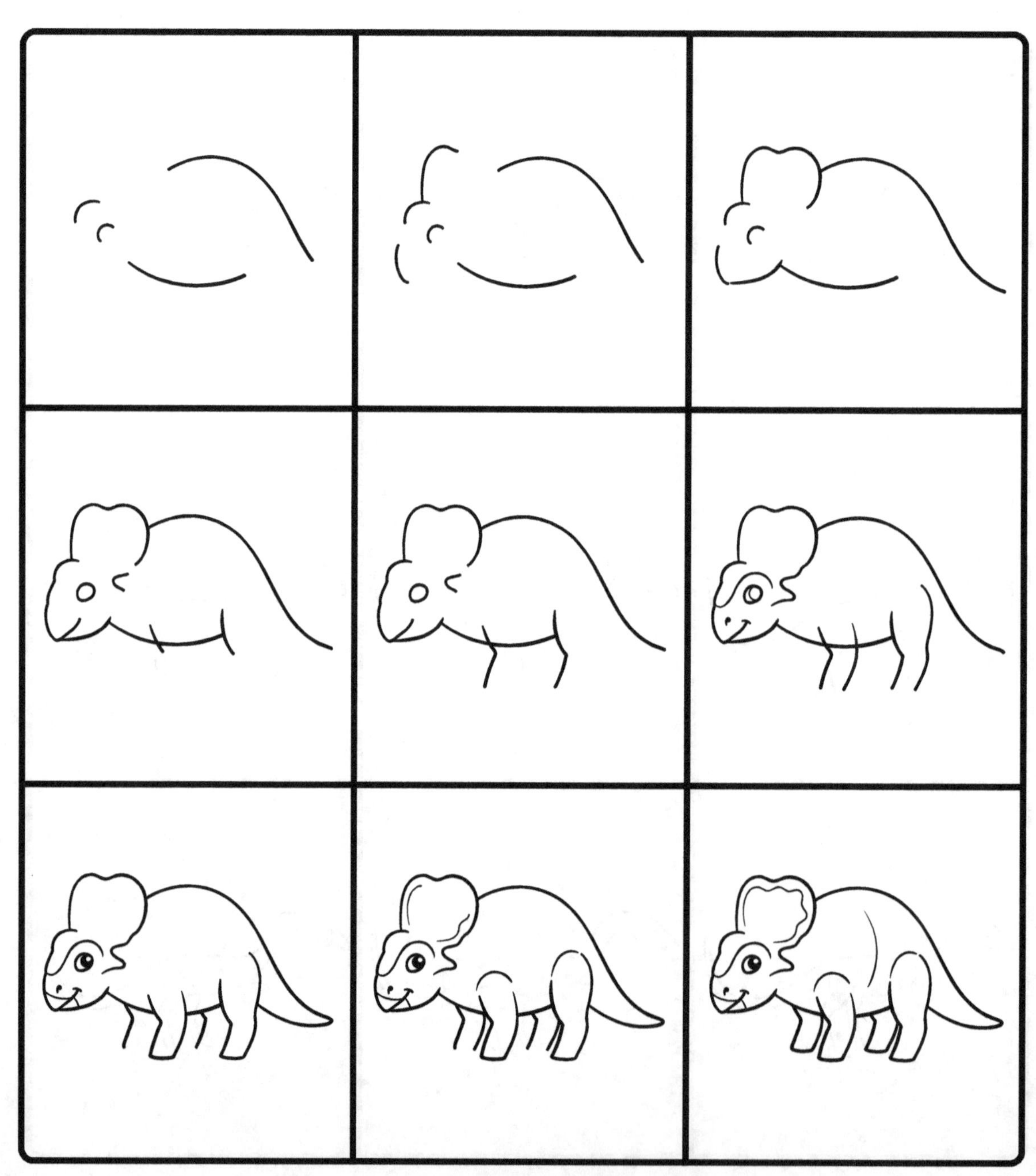

DIMETRODON

FACT:
ITS BIG SAIL IS LIKELY USED TO DEFEND ITSELF FROM PREDATORS, OR TO INTIMIDATE.

SIZE:
11 FEET – AS TALL AS A STANDING MOOSE.

ORIGIN:
NORTH AMERICA

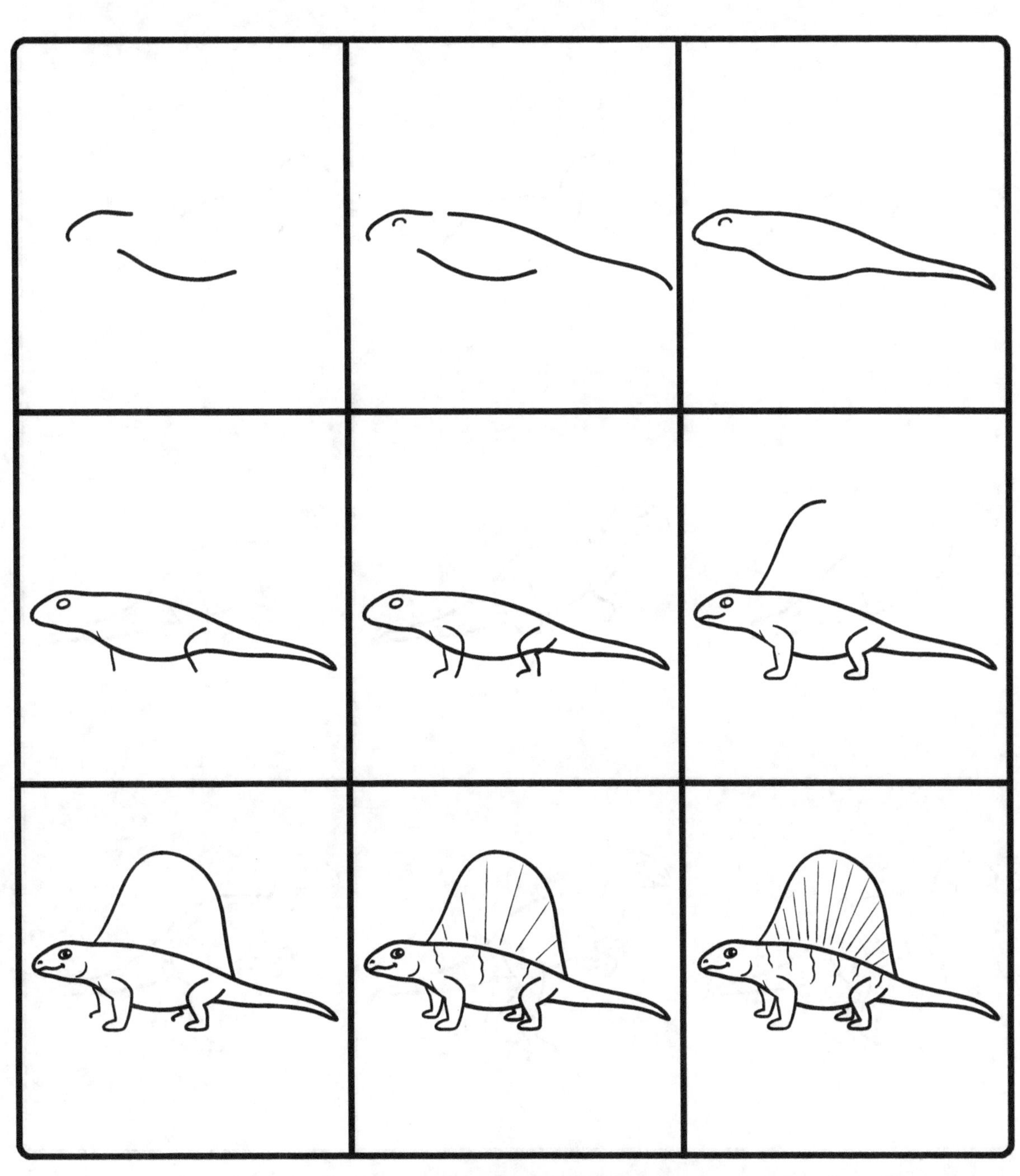

EDMONTOSAURUS

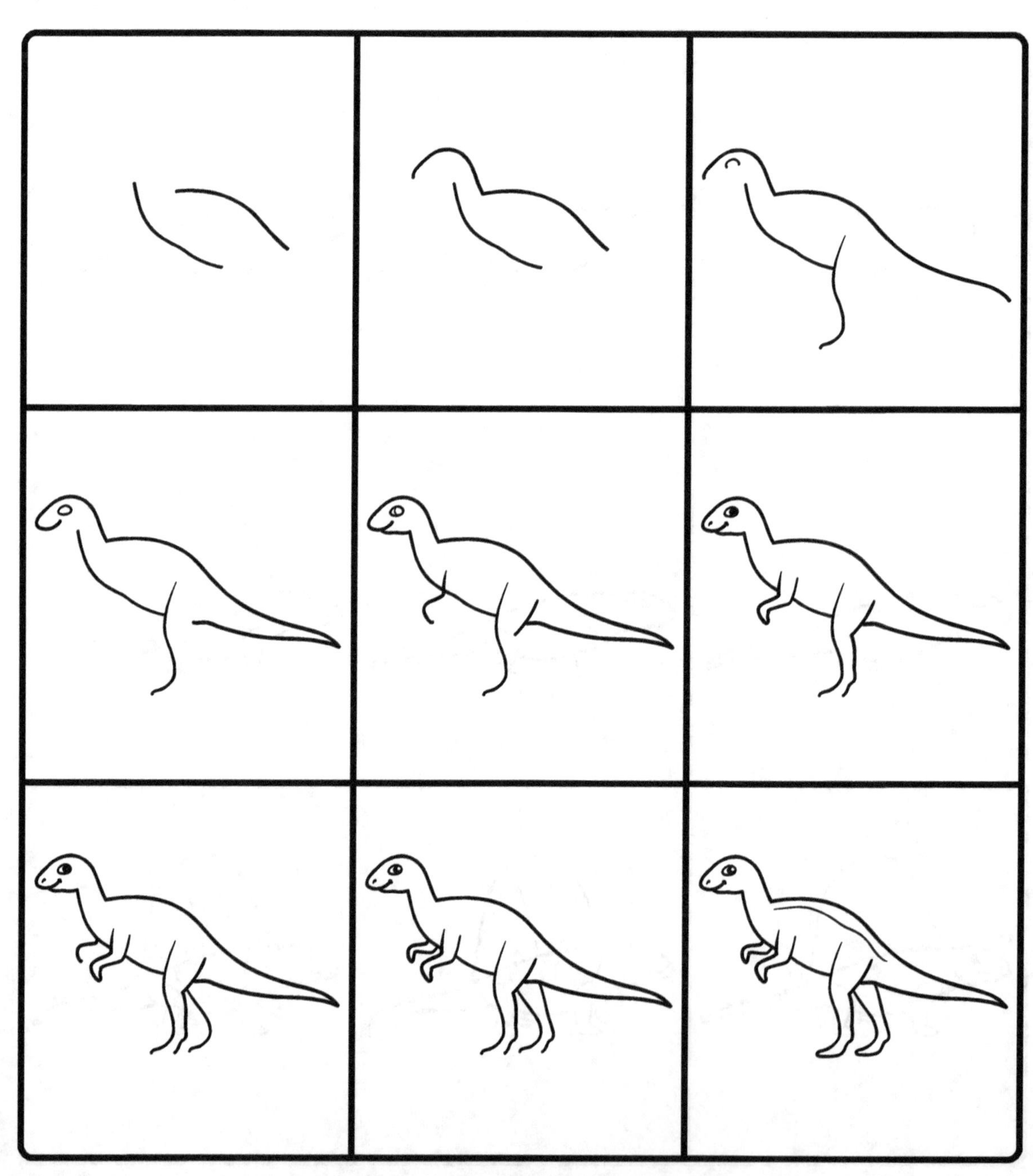

EORAPTOR

FACT:

PREFERS TO RUN THAN ATTACK.

SIZE:

1.5 FEET - AS BIG AS A DOG.

ORIGIN:

ARGENTINA.

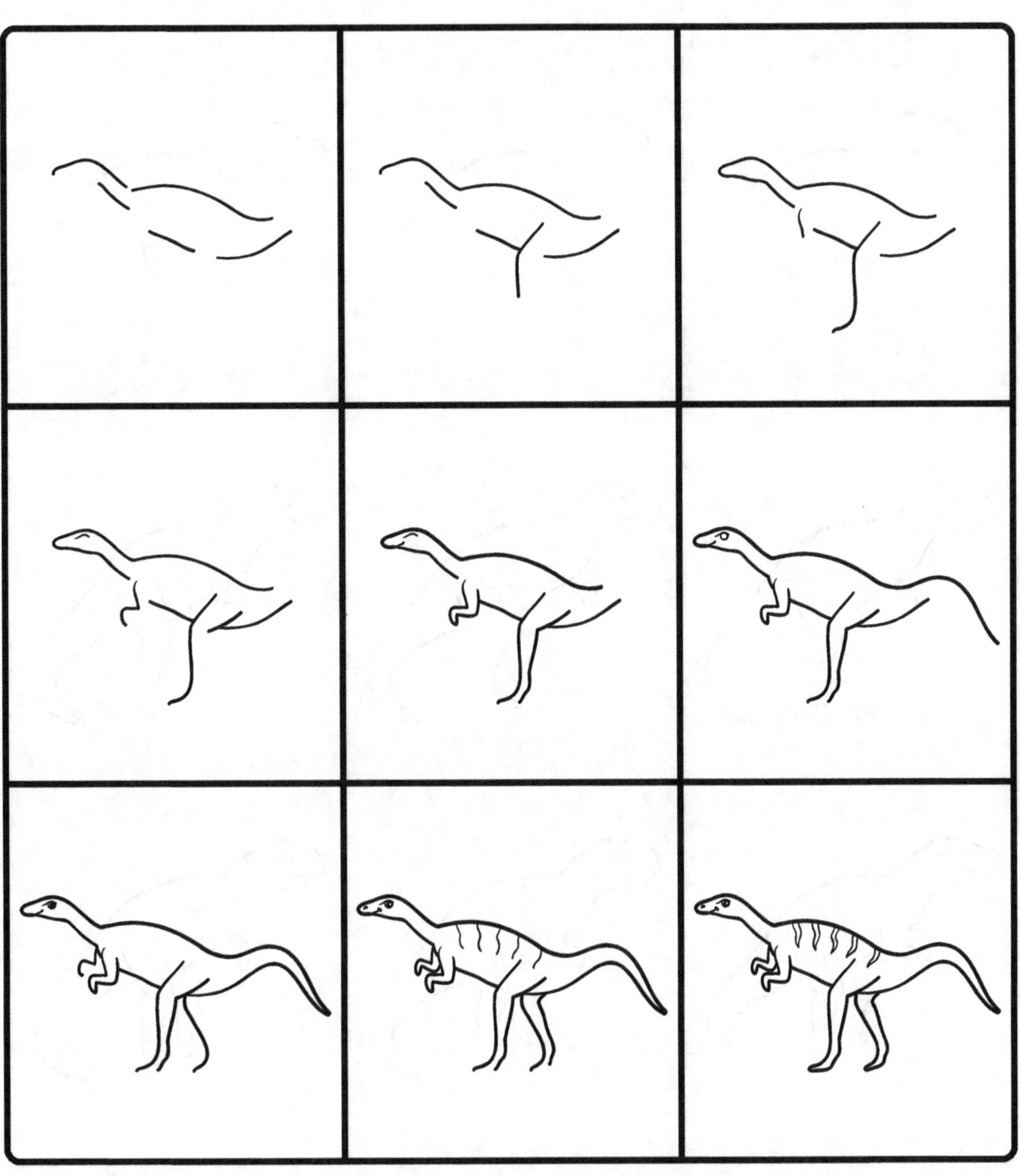

MEGALOSAURUS

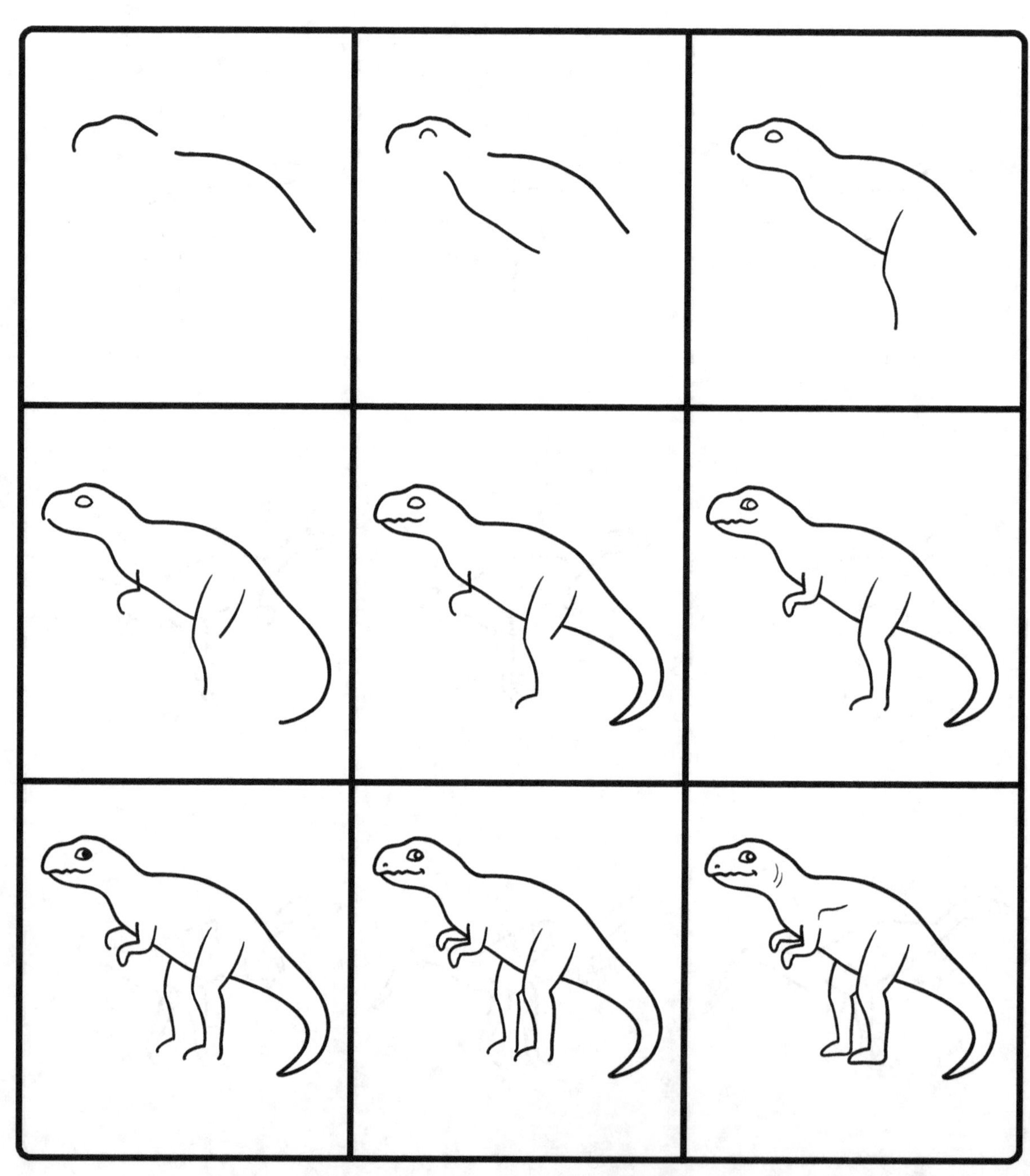

ARCHAEORNITHOMIMUS

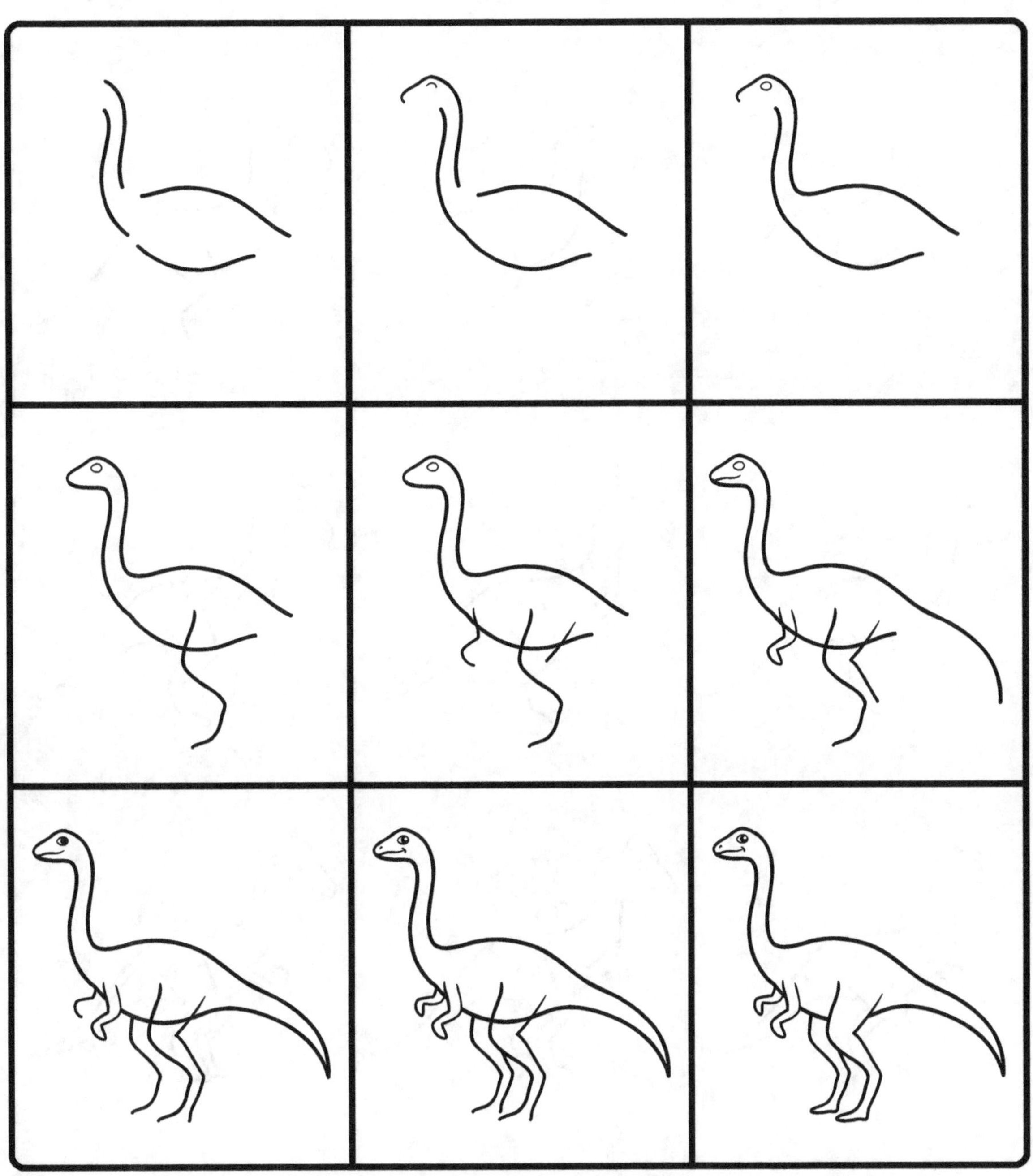

MAIASAURA

STAYS SAFE BY LIVING IN HERDS, AND CAN RUN FAST IN SHORT BURSTS.

SIZE:

30 FEET – AS LONG AS A GREEN ANACONDA.

ORIGIN:

MONTANA.

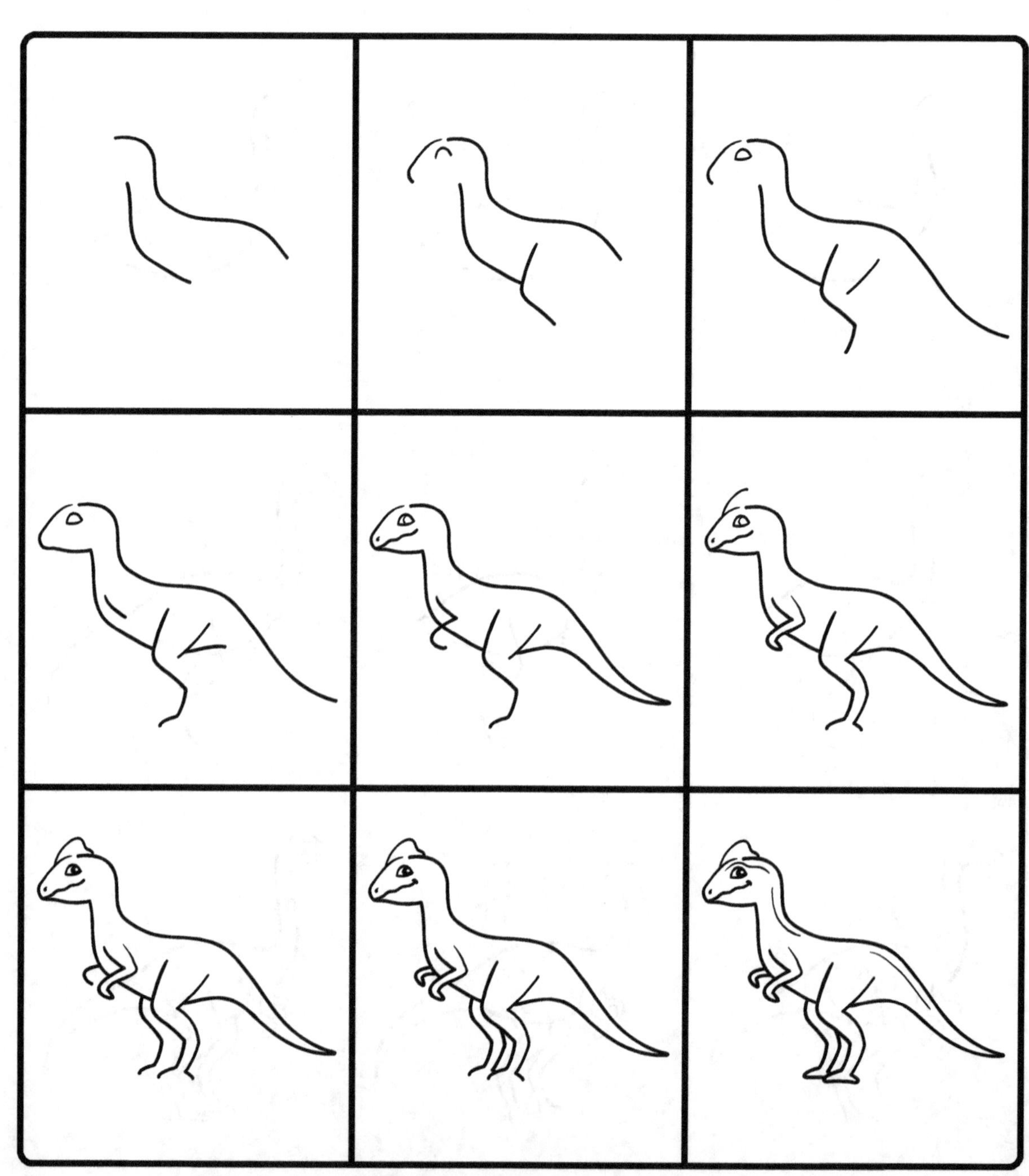

SAURONITHOLESTES

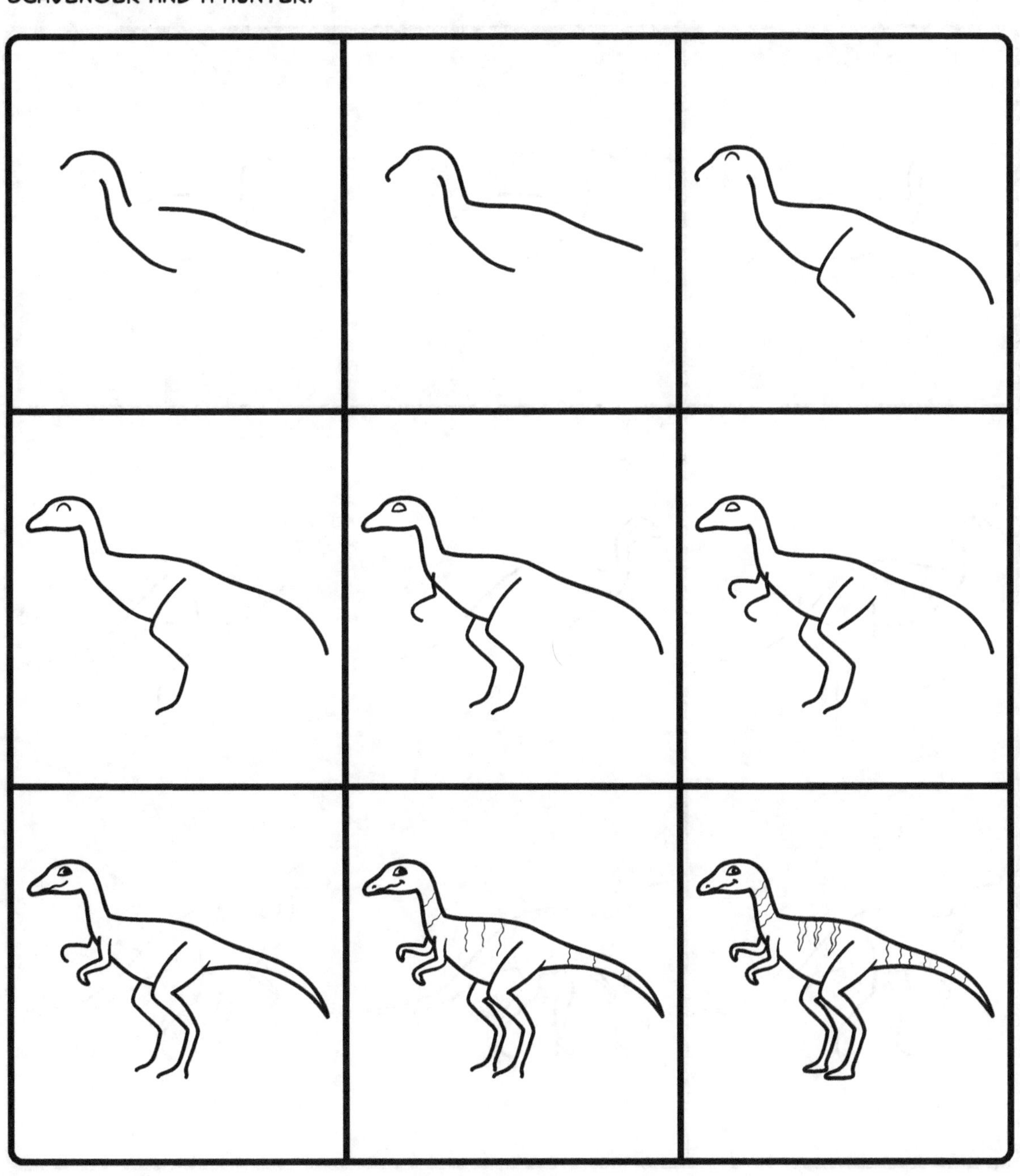

STENONYCHOSAURUS

HUNTED AND ATTACKED ITS PREY WITH ITS SICKLE-SHAPED CLAWS.

3 FEET – AS TALL AS AN ANTELOPE.

CANADA.

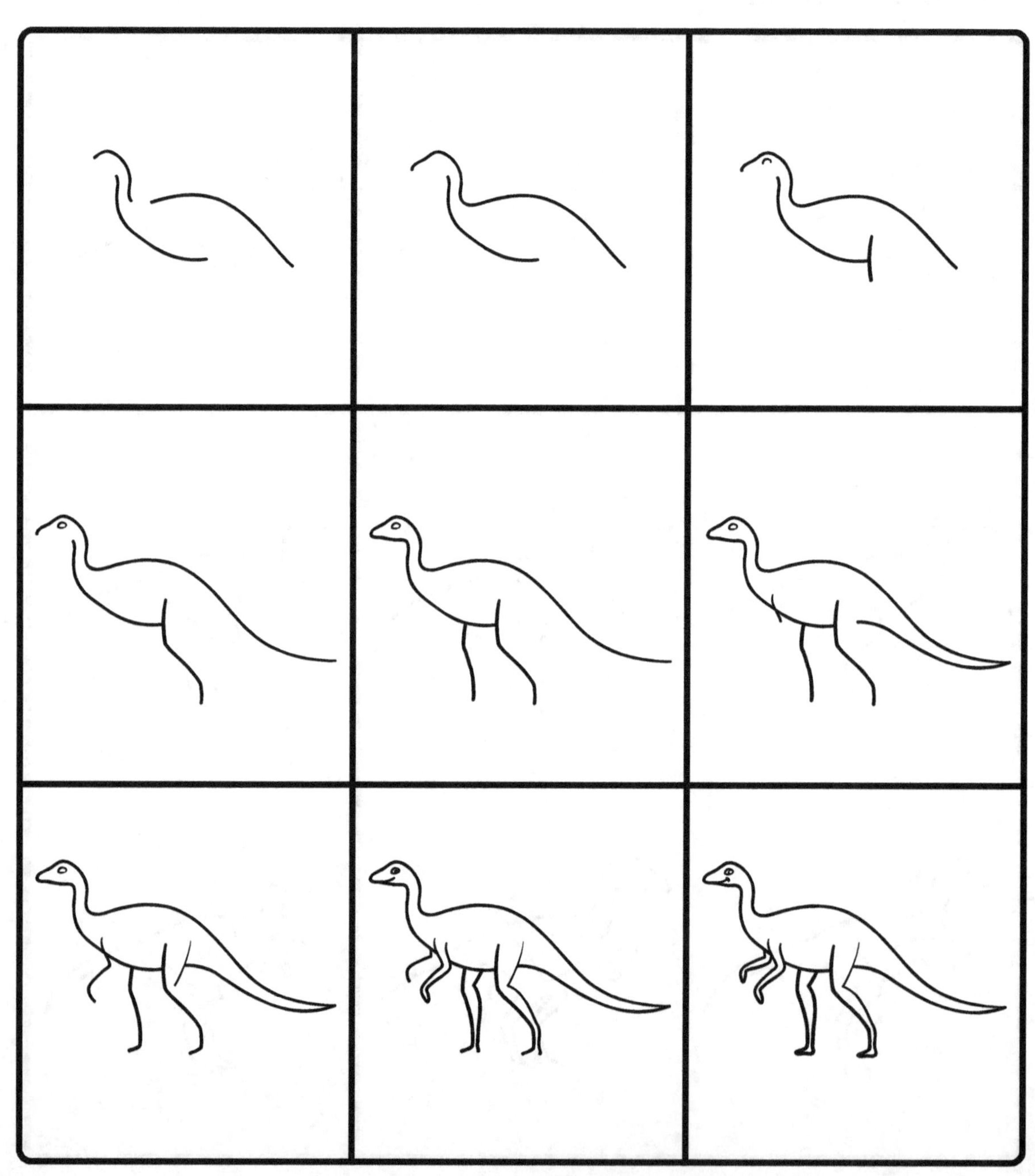

TYRANNOSAURUS

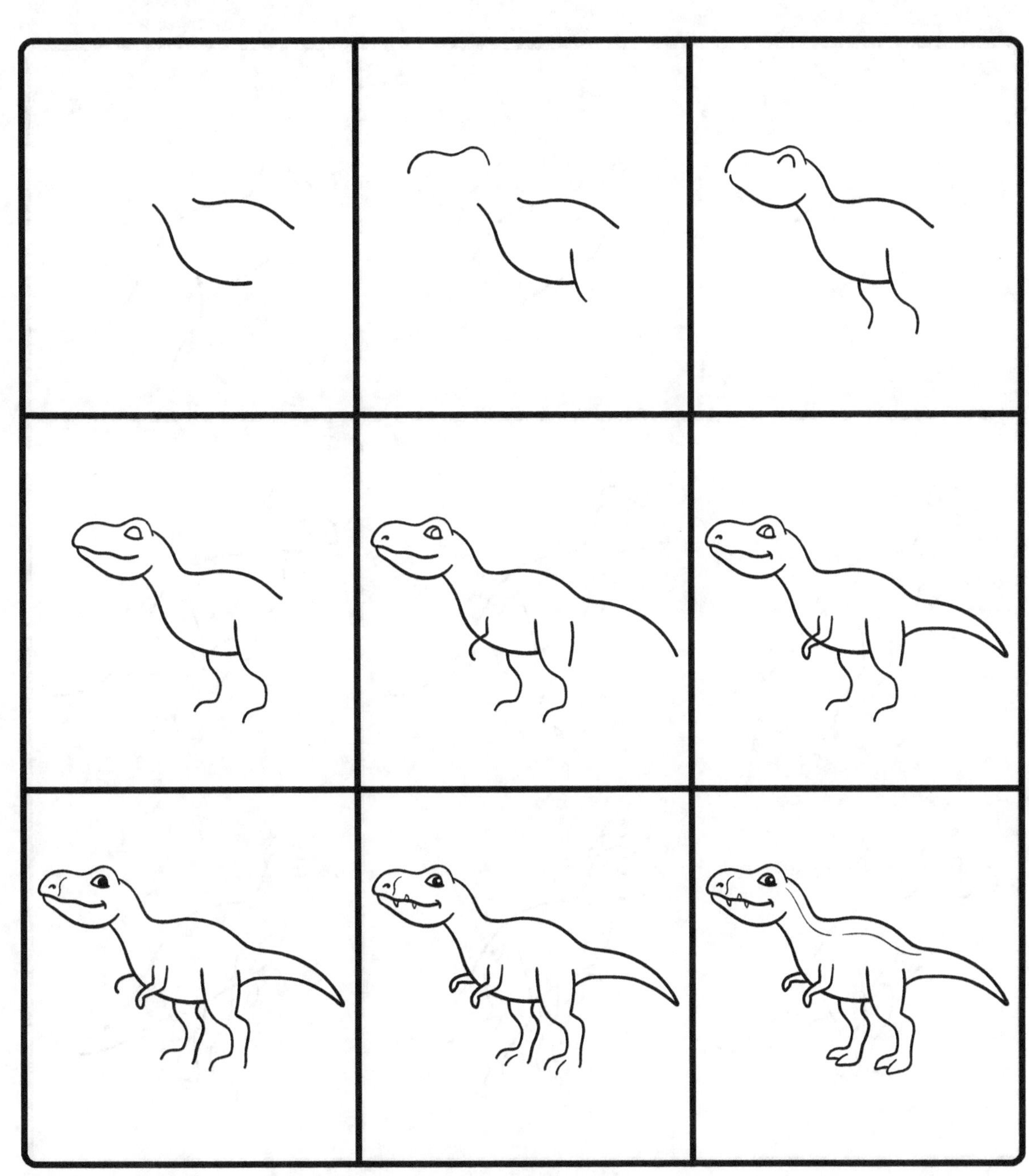

PACHYCEPHALOSAURUS

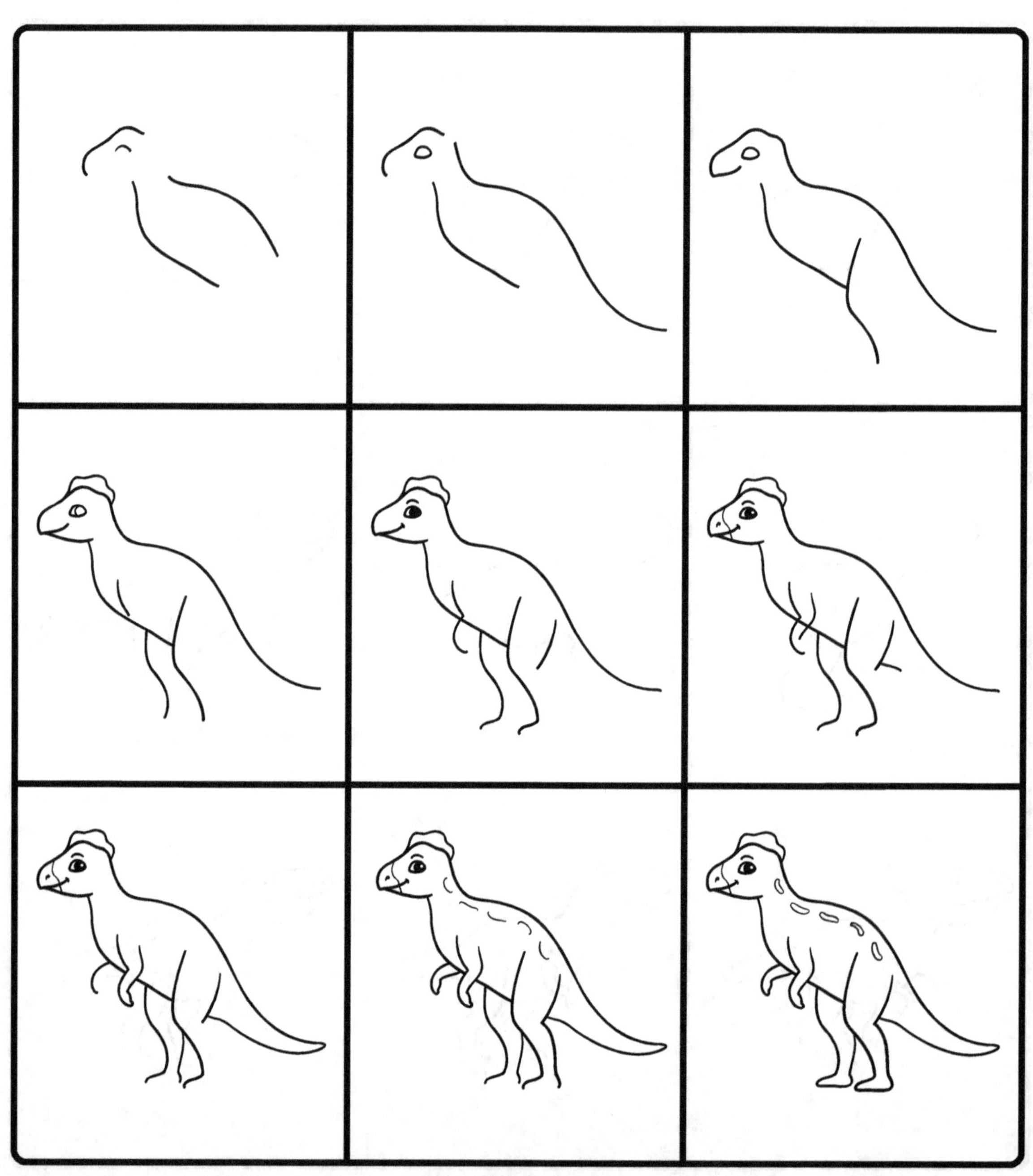

TRICERATOPS

FACT:
LIKELY USES ITS HORNS TO FEND OFF ATTACKS, TO FIGHT EACH OTHER, OR ATTRACT FEMALES.

SPEED:
15 MILES PER HOUR – AS FAST AS A KANGAROO.

ORIGIN:
NORTH AMERICA.

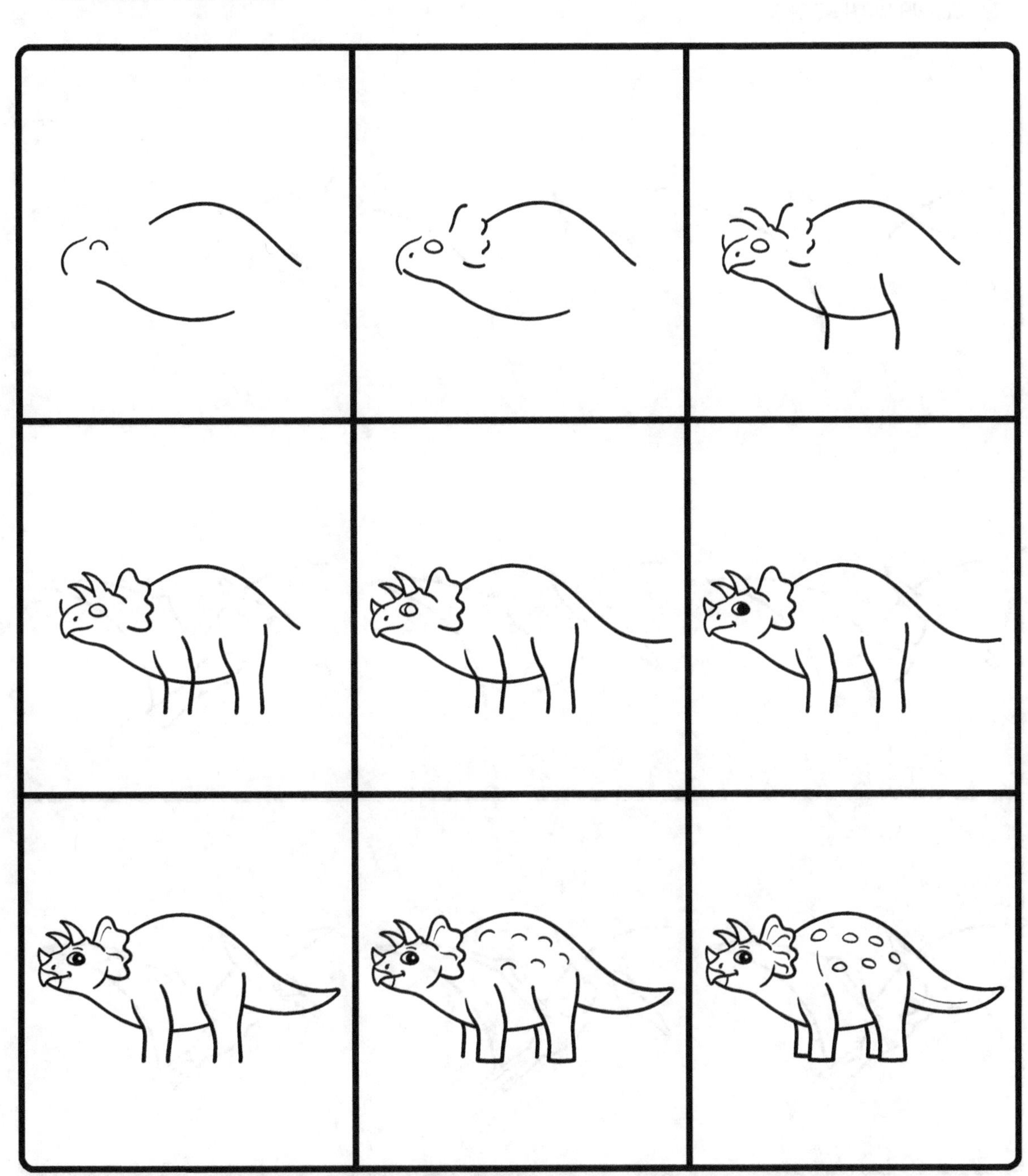

PTERODACTYL

SWOOPED DOWN ON ITS PREY FROM THE SKY, EATING MOSTLY FISH AND LITTLE ANIMALS WITH THEIR SHARP TEETH AND CLAWS WITH HOOKS.

35 FEET WIDE WINGSPAN - THE BIGGEST WAS THE SIZE OF A SMALL PLANE.

GERMANY.

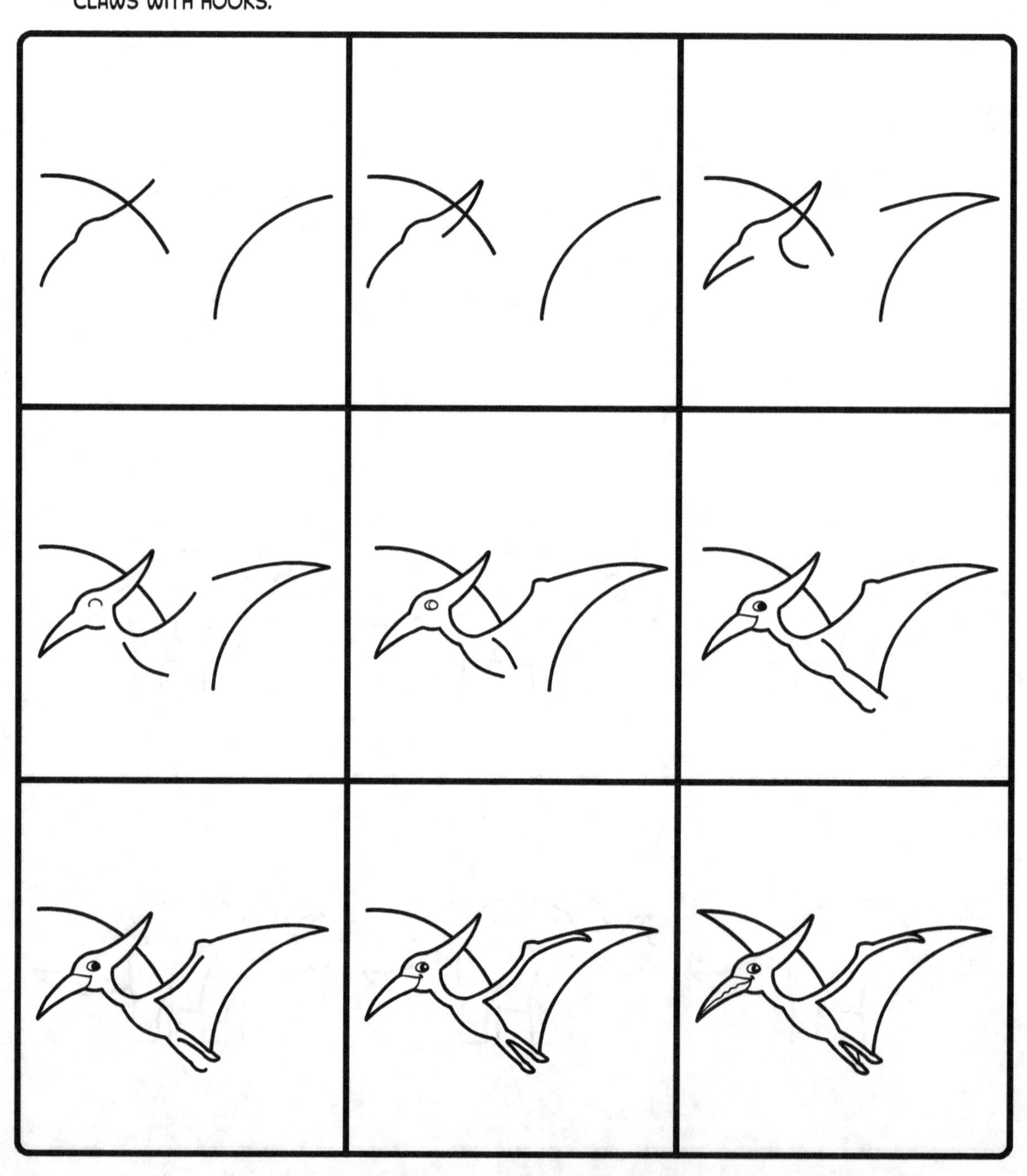

PLESIOSAUR

FACT:
ITS STRONG JAWS AND
LARGE SIZE HELPED IT
CATCH FISH AND OTHER
PREY IN THE SEA.

SIZE:
15 FEET - AS LONG AS A
LARGE ELEPHANT SEAL.

ORIGIN:
AUSTRALIA, ASIA, NORTH
AMERICA

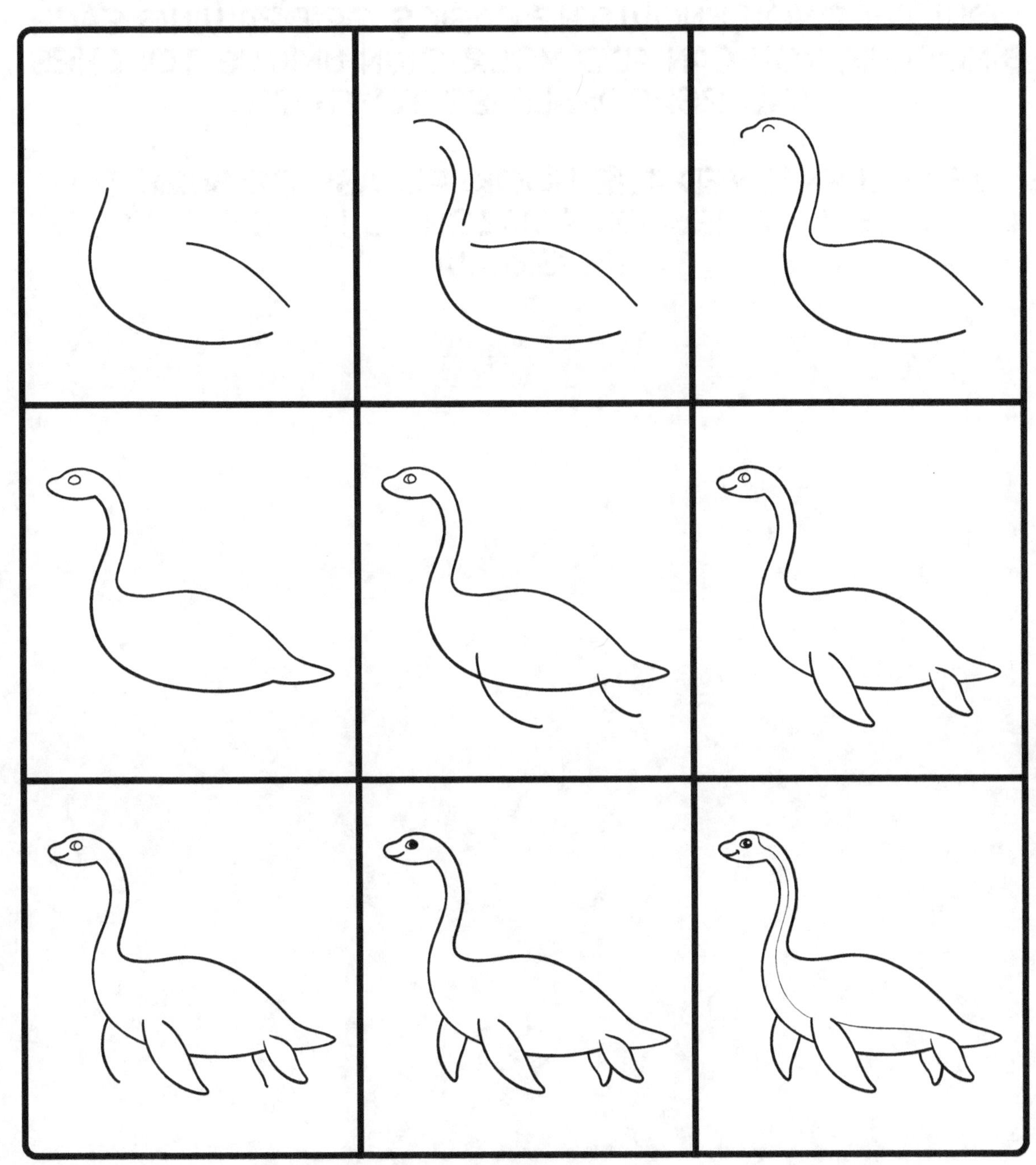

CONCLUSION

SO HOW DID YOU GO DRAWING THE DINOSAURS? WERE SOME DINOSAURS TRICKIER THAN OTHERS? OR SOME MORE FUN TO DRAW?

NOW THAT YOU KNOW THE BASICS OF DRAWING EACH DINOSAUR, YOU CAN ADD YOUR OWN UNIQUE TOUCHES AND PERSONALITIES TO THEM!

IF YOU ENJOYED THE BOOK, PLEASE BE SURE TO LEAVE US A REVIEW ON AMAZON AS IT REALLY HELPS US GROW!